BAGELS WITH BA

Babushka

Hilda Cohen

Front cover: The author (1932)

ISBN 0 906253 31 4

Photographs "Blackshirts" (Manchester Central Library)
Others from author's personal collection.

Typesetting Arena, 35 Parsonage Chambers, Manchester M3 2HN.

Printing L V Lawlor, Bottom O' Th Moor,
Huddersfield Road, Oldham.

Published jointly by Gatehouse Project
St Luke's, Sawley Road,
Miles Platting, Manchester M10 8DB.

and North West Shape
behind Shawgrove School, Cavendish Road,
West Didsbury, Manchester M20 8JR.

Distribution Gatehouse Project

Gatehouse Project is funded by the Government Inner Cities Programme and is a member of the Federation of Worker Writers and Community Publishers.

North West Shape is funded by North West Arts, the Association of Greater Manchester Authorities and Manchester City Council.

This publication has received financial support from North West Arts and Salford Cultural Services.

Bagels with Babushka

Foreword

Yesterday's action is obscured by today,
and the strongest link binding us to a
life constantly eaten away by forgetting
is nostalgia.

Milan Kundera

("The Joke" – Faber and Faber)

I've been writing for many years now, mostly for my own amusement and my family's. I joined a Creative Writing class at the College of Adult Education, All Saints, Manchester (now City College). There, under the guidance of tutors including a novelist and two poets, I have written memoirs and poetry. The memoirs were initially for my children and grandchildren.

Jim Burns, my present tutor, suggested I put them in chronological order and write an autobiography. I protested that this was too daunting. He firmly replied, "Then take it up to a certain age, or your marriage." I chose the latter option. It has been a therapeutic exercise. Thanks, Jim, for that initial push.

Through Steve Randall, I was put in touch with Rick Gwilt, an arts organiser with pensioners at North West Shape. It has been great fun working with Rick. There have been frequent dissensions during editorial sessions, arguments over syntax and tautology, but these have always been smoothed out amicably.

Thanks to Alison Burrows for typing up the manuscript, and of course to North West Shape and Gatehouse for jointly publishing the book.

Hilda Cohen
Blackley (North Manchester)
December 1988

1. Settlers in Salford

Sadie and Hilda

Some people claim to have residual memory of their birth. But my earliest memories go back to when I was three, living in a small terraced house in Fildes Street, in the Hightown area of Salford, with my mother and father and my sister, Sadie, who was a year older than me.

Our street was lost at one end in a maze of small streets, but led at the bottom end onto Marlborough Road. The elementary school there was attended by Sadie and me until we passed our scholarship to Summerhill School in Pendleton. In the late 20's this school was closed, and we transferred to Broughton High School.

I remember playing with Sadie under the kitchen table, which, covered with a long, overhanging cloth, created our own little world, a precursor of the Wendy house, our retreat from the intrusive adults who invaded the rest of the house.

One event which still perplexes me is a recollection of Sadie, who could be obstreperous, lying under the donkey-drawn cart of a rag-and-bone man, and being enticed out with some difficulty.

I have shadowy memories of my successor, Norah, born less than two years after me, who lived only a few short months. She died during an attack of convulsions. I asked one of my aunts why she had died. Her reply, 'She was too beautiful to live', sounded quite convincing at the time.

When I was six, my brother, Sidney was born. My mother's respite from child-bearing was due to my father's absence during the First World War. I cannot say he distinguished himself as a soldier. He served his time in non-combative duties, in the cookhouse. His mother and father were naturalised Germans, and the surname of Lichtenstein no doubt contributed to his relegation to this role. He never showed any aptitude for, nor interest in cooking when we were at home but strangely enough, when he was old and living alone, he began to cook as a hobby. He then spoke of cookery as an art form. Florence Greenberg, or at any rate her cookbook, was his constant companion, and his annotated copy, with remarks like 'not enough sugar' or 'use less eggs' on some of the recipes, has travelled round my family over the years.

My father's parents, Jeanette and Gustav, left Germany in 1890 with four children. Almost as soon as she set foot in Dover, Jeanette gave birth to my father, Frederick, thus bestowing on him British citizenship. They settled in Manchester, where eventually they had four more children, four sons and five daughters in all.

My mother's parents escaped from the pogroms in Russia and also made their home in Manchester. My Russian grandmother's name was Leah Lazarus. I never knew my Russian grandfather. He died before I was born. Leah, whom we called Bobby, a diminutive of Babushka, Russian for grandmother, was left a widow with six children, three boys and three girls, to bring up single-handed. My mother, Minnie was the eldest child.

I was told by a cousin at some point in my youth that my mother and father had had a shot-gun wedding. The Lichtensteins hadn't been pleased about the union, but my mother's pregnancy had settled the issue. However, my Aunt Flo had already told me that the mother of the cousin who imparted the information had married for the same reason.

There was no social contact between the Lazaruses and the Lichtensteins, except a cool relationship with my mother, her in-laws regarding themselves a cut above the Lazaruses. Certainly they were more literate, both reading and writing fluently in English. Grandpa became quite an avid reader of English literature. But Bobby often lapsed into Yiddish, especially when talking to her contemporaries. And no-one ever helped to teach her to read, although she told Sadie and me she would like to do so.

At school, one day, we were presented with commemorative mugs and bags of caramels. It was to celebrate the Armistice. My sister and I hurried home with our trophies and were delighted to find our father there. I was quite hurt when he refused one of my sticky offerings in favour of one of Sadie's sweets, which she had managed to keep in an edible condition.

When we were considered old enough, Sadie and I used to visit Granny and Grandpa in their house in Marlborough Road. Flo, their unmarried daughter, lived with them. She was regarded as a mischiefmaker by the rest of the family, and whilst being warned to be careful what we revealed or did on these visits by our mother, we were closely questioned on our return home, as to what had been said and done by the Lichtensteins.

Opposite their house was the Co-op, where we bought coconut biscuits with holes in the centre, made at the Co-op biscuit works which then flourished in Crumpsall. I was intrigued sometimes to see a horse-drawn cart standing outside the butchery department, loaded with huge slabs of dripping ice. If no-one was looking, you could sometimes find slivers of ice to suck.

Granny was a small, neat person with a mild manner. She had a pointed chin and several moles on her face. I wondered whether she had any teeth, but one did not explore grandmothers' mouths in those days, nor ask them rude questions. She usually wore black. A sepia wedding photograph of her and Grandpa that hung in the kitchen, with her seated and him standing behind her with a proprietorial air, showed them to have been an attractive couple when they were young. Grandpa was still quite striking, but I did not like the feel of his beard when he sat me on his knee and put his face close to mine. Granny looked splendid on the rare occasions when she went out. She wore a long black skirt over a rustling taffeta underskirt, a black cape with jet beads sewn on it, a demure bonnet and black gloves.

Flo was permanently "on the sick", though she was secretive about what kind of work she had done to qualify for this benefit. She was most unprepossessing in appearance, with her angular frame, long nose and sallow complexion. Her voice droned on monotonously and complainingly all the time. Mrs. Shapiro next door distinguished herself by making real coffee. Most people aspired only to Camp coffee in those days. It came in bottles like H.P. sauce and was liberally laced with chicory. When the fragrant aroma of Mrs. Shapiro's coffee wafted over, sometimes Flo would say to Sadie and me, "Come on, let's go and have a cup of coffee with Mrs Shapiro!" and, uninvited and rather apprehensive (at least Sadie and I) we would appear just as the lady was about to have her elevenses. The look of resignation on her face suggested that she was not unaccustomed to this occurrence, and she would invite us to have a drink with her.

There was great excitement when our French cousin, Yvonne, came to stay with Granny for a few weeks. Her father had been killed during the war. (Yvonne herself was widowed in the Second World War when the Germans invaded Paris.) I was envious when my grandmother told me that Yvonne liked chocolate sandwiches. This seemed a big improvement on the cheese or jam sandwiches I had at home, but the idea was coolly received by my mother when I suggested it to her.

Bobby lived in a mean little two-up-and-down house in Peter Street, a few minutes walk away from our house. You stepped through the front door straight into the parlour, where Uncle Mark, her bachelor son, played cards right through Saturday night with his cronies.

Sometimes we went there on Sunday morning to find them having their breakfast – strong tea, thickly buttered black bread and salt herrings or kippers. Once I was sent for some herrings to one of the little immigrant shops on Waterloo Road. They sold tempting delicacies like smetana and kess, (sour cream and a kind of cottage cheese). Barrels of pickled cucumbers and brine-soaked herrings stood on the floor. I held the herrings, wrapped in newspaper under my arm, and found on my return to Peter Street that one had slithered out of its inadequate wrapping somewhere on the road back from the shop.

Unlike Granny's house, which was always neat and tidy, Bobby's, even to our uncritical eyes, was untidy and shabby.

Bobby had none of the smart trinkets that Granny Lichtenstein possessed. Indoors she always wore the traditional cotton overall that covered her completely and fastened at the back with tapes. She went out in a nondescript coat, her head covered with a scarf, peasant-fashion. Whenever she saw us, her face lit up in a great gum-revealing smile. But even without teeth, she enjoyed her bagels, dipping them in her tea, and she seemed to have no problems with her food. She made a kind of puree of apples by scraping them with a knife. She was a good cook and produced mouth-watering kuchen, a sort of fruit loaf, delicious when eaten spread with butter. Her chicken, roasted in chicken fat and seasoned with bay leaves and pepper corns, even tempted me, a most finnicky eater. All her cooking was done in an old black-leaded oven. Bobby, like Granny, had an unmarried daughter still living at home. Jane worked in a clothing factory and was tired and irritable when she came home at night. After the war Mark, unemployed and becoming increasingly deaf, bickered with her, and Bobby was often the target for their joint dissatisfaction. During the war he had worked as a night porter at the Midland Hotel, and he used to bring Sadie and me left-overs from the dances and functions there, beautiful paper hats, capes made of crepe paper, encrusted with spangles, Spanish mantillas and tortoise-shell combs – glittering prizes they seemed to us. He often brought us food when my father was in the army.

Bobby's other two sons were Lionel, who worked in a clothing factory and whom we rarely saw, and Benny, who was an engineer, quite unusual for a Jew at that time. He used to tell me that, when I was older, people would travel as freely in aeroplanes as they then did by tram, bus and train. Betsy, the other daughter, and my mother had quite a close relationship. They both found Jane rather difficult to handle.

My father's brothers and sisters seemed more formidable to me. My father and his two brothers, William and Benjamin, went into tailoring. The clothing business was one of the chief sources of employment open to Jews then. But Louis, the other brother, emigrated to America, becoming a lawyer and eventually a judge. The family lost track of him after some years. He came to a party to celebrate the birth of my brother when we lived in Great Cheetham Street – this was before he emigrated – and left a photo of himself as a souvenir. I was troubled some time later when I went into the kitchen to see my mother kissing his photograph. Neither of us said anything.

My father's sisters were Marie, Pauline, Ray, Annie and Flo. He insisted that Flo had been dropped on her head as a child, and this accounted for her erratic behaviour. They were rather overbearing and arrogant in their manner. With the exception of Flo, they were quite versatile. Marie was a dancer and appeared with the Tiller girls, a well-known dancing troupe, before she went to France, where she married a Frenchman. Pauline sang for a time with the Carla Rosa Opera Company, probably in the chorus. She went to America and later became a Christian Scientist. The family was perplexed by this deviation. She compounded it by sending tracts to them from time to time. I once went into a Christian Science Reading Room in Manchester to read and ponder, but found myself unconvinced by what I read there. Ray emigrated to South Africa. She was a volatile, difficult woman, whose thwarted personal ambitions were later channelled into promoting the career of her daughter, who showed great promise as a pianist.

After his return home from the war, my father set up in business as a merchant tailor in Deansgate, and we moved to a better house in Great Cheetham Street. There was one drawback. A lady of indeterminate age was already in residence and occupied the sitting room and one of the bedrooms. A condition of the tenancy was that she retained these rooms and had the use of the kitchen and bathroom. I do not remember the manner of her going, but she seemed to disappear from the scene quite suddenly.

I was not a strong child and I remember the alarm I felt during a rare school medical examination when I read the comment, "Weak", against the question, "State of Health?" Sometimes when I was running a temperature, my father used to produce a bottle of Fennings Fever Cure, in which he seemed to have inordinate faith, and bribe me with sixpence to have a spoonful. I loathed the taste of it, but could not resist the money. Scotts Emulsion, a white viscous liquid, was always used as a prophylactic when winter approached. We preferred cod liver oil and malt, with the fishy taste masked in its toffee-like base.

2. From Lichtenstein to Leach

My mother had suffered for many years from duodenal ulcers. Privation in childhood and poverty during the war had undermined her health. I see her now, as in a camera shot, silhouetted in the kitchen doorway, rigid, a spasm of pain masking her face. As my father's business prospered, he bought her new furniture and carpets for the home. She looked at them sadly and said, "I'll not live to enjoy them!" I stored this remark, undigested, in my child's brain. It was too hard to accept.

One day Sadie and I returned home from school to find the house full of mourning relations. Bobby wailed and beat her breast. My mother had been rushed to hospital with peritonitis and had died. She was thirty and my grandmother's favourite child. Sadie and I, stunned and uncomprehending, were sent from the stricken house to wheel Sydney, in his trolley, round Mandley Park. To our lasting regret, she did not leave us a single photograph of herself.

That night my distraught father slept with my sister and I in our double bed in the back bedroom, with Sydney in his cot. The gas jet flared and flickered fitfully, a fan of blue light radiating from a small orange sun. The gas mantle, which normally curbed the unruly jet and shed a white radiance had broken. Frightened and miserable, my sister and I cried and woke up our young brother. My father, for the first time in his life, smacked us.

Bobby moved in with Janey to look after us. Since our mother's death Janey had a very protective attitude towards us.

After the funeral we were off school for a couple of weeks while we recovered from shock and the household was reassembled. I discovered, on my return to school, that my class had done some new work in arithmetic. Each Monday morning, we found as we entered the classroom that sums had been set on the blackboard to keep the class occupied while the class teacher, Miss Durbury, got on with registration and other tasks. I looked at the sums and flinched. Miss Durbury was a virago of a woman, disliked and feared throughout the school. That particular morning, her work accomplished, she proceeded on a tour of inspection to see how her charges were performing. Her strident voice reverberated as she took to task the unfortunates who had made mistakes. This, coupled with her unruly hands, ensured that she never had problems with class discipline! Suddenly I was taken by surprise to receive a vicious thump in the back because of my ineptitude in tackling the work. When I went home to lunch and told my aunt what had happened, she was furious. She returned with me to school in the afternoon and loudly berated the teacher, in front of the class. She told her that if she ever laid hands on me again, there would be serious repercussions. The class sat back and relished the spectacle. I had no more trouble with Miss Durbury after that incident. Some time later, I succumbed to a childish ailment and, while I was recuperating, walked past the school. I heard her from the street, screaming at some victim in our classroom, and thanked God from the bottom of my heart for granting me a respite from her. Years later I learned that she had been certified as insane. I wondered how many children's minds she had scarred during her years as a teacher.

After a year of terror with Miss Durbury, it was sheer bliss to move into Miss Wall's class. Her voice was "low and sweet, an excellent thing in woman". She had golden hair and was most attractive in appearance. It is possible I exaggerated Miss Wall's beauty and saw her through a myopic haze. My mother had long ignored postcards she received, telling her that I was suffering from defective vision and inviting me to go to the school clinic to have my eyes tested. A year or so later, I got glasses and a new world was revealed to me, crystal-clear and cruel in its clarity. Nevertheless, Miss Wall was a very amiable person. She instilled in the girls that the hallmark of a lady was always to (a) wear a hat, (b) wear or carry gloves, and (c) have clean shoes. In that case I was never likely to qualify. I could never find a hat I liked to fit me, having thick, unruly hair. Gloves were too expensive an item, as I invariably lost one or both whenever I went out. I did, however, try to please her by having reasonably clean shoes.

But at home things weren't going too well. Unfortunately, Bobby and Janey had rather primitive ideas about housekeeping, not up to my father's expectations. Also, it became clear that Bobby was hoping that Janey would eventually fill my mother's place in the household. So, after some months, Bobby and Janey had to go. They packed up their belongings and returned to their own home and Mark. There did not seem to be any acrimony in this outcome to the venture.

Their places in our household were filled by my father's mother and

Aunt Flo, Grandfather Lichtenstein having died some time before. Granny was a very good housekeeper and, with Flo's help, ran the household smoothly. Flo, however, was immature and quarrelsome. After disagreements she always demanded apologies, which Sadie and I were reluctant to give, because we often felt that the troubles were of her making. My grandmother was the peacemaker on these occasions, intervening in our arguments and trying to placate the adversaries. Sometimes she received blows from Flo intended for us. My brother, Sydney, was younger and more biddable and usually managed to keep out of domestic disputes.

There was at that time a shop in Cheetham village that sold hand-made chocolates, which Flo, Sadie and I visited every Sunday morning. Ignoring the boys and girls engaged in their ritual walk up and down Cheetham Hill Road, we made our way to the chocolate shop near the top end of Waterloo road, drooling with anticipation. Our favourites were coffee creams, but sometimes we bought caramels or chocolates with marzipan fillings. Sadie and I linked Flo all the way home as she doled out the chocolates. I cannot recall any bickering on these outings.

One occasion when she took me out was up to then my most embarrassing experience. She told me we were going to a Mrs. Radivan, who lived in Cheetham, for our tea. Being wise to Flo's wiles by this time, I asked her whether we were expected. 'No!' was the reply. 'But it'll be all right!' It was evident when we arrived at Mrs. Radivan's that she was not pleased. There was a battle of wills. She was determined not to offer us anything in the way of refreshment, but Flo had no intention of leaving without it. They talked in a desultory way. I fidgeted in my seat. At long last, the poor woman admitted defeat. She said to Flo, 'You wouldn't like to stay to tea, would you?' Flo intimated we would. I didn't enjoy the meal.

Every Sunday Flo wrote long letters to members of her family living abroad, cataloguing her grievances against my father and his ungrateful family. Sadie and I often tried to read her outpourings, but she never left her epistles uncovered long enough for us to get more than a quick glimpse of the contents. She would not allow Bobby to visit us, and did all she could to discourage us from seeing her.

Life with Flo gradually inured us to her oddness. But sometimes it was embarrassing to find that she was not quite as others. One day she allowed Sadie and me to have a joint birthday party. Our birthdays were within ten days of each other. We sat round a table with our friends partaking of the spread she had provided. We heard her voice rumbling down the passage as she went into the kitchen, talking to grannie. Suddenly, one of the children said, 'There's a ghost in this house!' The party atmosphere was shattered for me as our friends laughed and pretended to be frightened.

Some of her eating habits fascinated me. She was fond of Skipper sardines which she smothered with H.P. sauce. I didn't like sardines, but she ate them with such relish that I decided that I might eat them when I was older. She was addicted to bananas, and unfurled them lika a monkey and nibbled away until she came to the end, when she folded up and discarded the skin.

I remember once when my pertness must have really annoyed her. She was ironing at the time. She chased me upstairs, still holding the small hand iron. I reached the safety of the lavatory and locked myself in until the iron and her temper had cooled down. There were no recriminations when I ventured downstairs. Granny must have intervened.

One day at school the headmistress came into the classroom with some documents which she discussed with the class teacher. When she left the room, the teacher told me to stand up and announced to the class that my name had been changed by deed poll and in future I was to be known as Hilda Leach. This was a complete surprise to me. My father and his brothers made the change-over together, having decided that a German name was not an asset in the business world, with memories of the war still in people's minds. They accepted their positions as merchant tailors, but my father, a frustrated academic, never fitted into that role.

Sadie and I passed the scholarship and transferred to Summerhill School on Eccles Old Road. A group of us travelled by bus and we diverted ourselves by snatching each other's gloves and hats and throwing them out of the upper windows en route. The unfortunate owner had to alight at the next stop to retrieve her possessions. Sometimes when we got off the bus at Mandley Park we would find Bobby patiently waiting for us. She would take us to the sweet shop across the road, and to our embarrassment, say to the shopkeeper, 'I want a quarter of the best chocolates for my grandchildren'. Once, for our birthday, she gave us a brown paper parcel. On opening it at home, we found it contained two bedspreads, one lemon-coloured and the other orange-coloured. She could ill-afford them. They survived her life-time and became, for me, a symbol of her deep love that sustained us during our motherless childhood.

Sometimes we went to visit Bobby. We felt self-conscious in our school uniforms, having to run the gauntlet of the inquisitive, not always friendly eyes of people standing in their front doorways. Street doors were kept ajar, so that the occupants were always aware of any interesting incidents that might occur in their street theatre – there was no television to divert them in those days. At one particular house, I sometimes caught sight of a beautiful young girl, a flower blossoming in an arid desert. To avoid the battery of disconcerning eyes, we occasionally went through the back entries. Here one had to step warily to avoid the excrement of dogs and cats. Often we arrived to find Bobby holding court in her little domain. Our entrance was the signal for the rapid dispersal of the old ladies. Our grandmother would clasp her hands ecstactically and say, 'I wouldn't change places with the Queen of England!' 'Neither would she with you!' I'd smartly reply. Often the cupboard was bare and she would send us out to the shops for cakes and smetana and kess, and watch us lovingly as we ate.

After grandmother and Flo had been with us for some time, we heard that the husband of an aunt, who lived in America, had died, leaving her with two daughters about the same age as my sister and myself. Heart-rending letters had been received, telling us of their straitened circumstances, and it was arranged that they were to come for an indefinite period, perhaps eventually to settle in England. Our poor relations duly arrived – with mountains of luggage. My sister and I were green with envy when we saw our cousins' extensive wardrobes and compared their beautiful dresses with ours. Because our house only possessed three bedrooms, the girls had to share a bedroom with my sister and me. For some unknown reason, the advent of new blood in the vicinity encouraged some bugs, which had previously lain dormant in the cracks and crevices of our bedroom wallpaper, to make exploratory raids on our American cousins.

Their howls of anguish and distress in the night brought their mother into the bedroom. She was outraged. We had the room fumigated and the bugs were vanquished. Aunt Annie was very strict and insisted that Lois and Alfreda sat at table with ramrod-straight backs. Aunt Flo was furious at the amount of milk they imbibed at breakfast

– the milk-drinking craze was at its height in America – and told Sadie and me that we must get up early and drink our share of milk. As we normally drank tea, we resisted this attempt to make us fellow-conspirators in the battle of beverages. In the deteriorating situation, Aunt Annie, who had previously been one of the recipients of Flo's missives about our misdeeds, became a target for Flo's wrath. The situation became exacerbated to such an extent that Aunt and cousins moved on to another relative before they finally returned home for good. After a decent interval, letter-writing was resumed and fresh grievances aired.

One of the tasks Flo jibbed at was cleaning the front doorstep. Not to have a clean doorstep was considered a sign of sloth in Lancashire in those days. One day, in an unguarded moment, I offered to do it for her. I warmed to my task, smoothly applied the stone, embellishing the border with a darker tone. The donkey stone used was obtained from the rag-and-bone man, who haunted the vicinity in search of rags and cast-off clothes. He also offered blown-up balloons, but these were considered suspect, having been blown up by men who might harbour germs. Flo praised me lavishly and I found myself encumbered with this task, until I staged a rebellion.

3. The House in Northumberland Street

As my father's business prospered, it was decided that we should move to a bigger house in Northumberland Street. Although only about half a mile away, it was in a much more salubrious neighbourhood. There was a large drawing-room where I did my homework in years to come, warming my chilblained toes in the winter with a one-bar electric fire; where I was compelled to practise my violin, screeching away out of earshot of my unappreciative brother and sister; and where fifty guests celebrated my wedding some years later. There was a dining room, a cloak room and an enormous kitchen. Sliding cupboards lined one wall, and I remember a game of hide-and-seek played by an impudent mouse with my father, as he pursued it from cupboard to cupboard, brandishing a poker, frantically sliding doors to and fro. His language matched his behaviour.

Upstairs there were four bedrooms. The lavatory, bath and wash-basin were in three small separate rooms. There were large cellars. One had been used as a games room by the previous occupants and contained a billiard table. This we later removed to the kitchen. Another cellar was used for doing the weekly wash, traditionally on Monday. To me it was a horrible ritual, the whole house damp and reeking of wet washing when I came home from school. The water was heated in a boiler over a coal fire which burned smokily throughout most of the day. There was an old-fashioned mangle which had to be laboriously turned by hand and a dolly tub in which the clothes were vigorously agitated. The little blue-bag was a must to make sheets, shirts, blouses and tableclothes whiter than white. Cottons had to be starched so that they could be ironed into sleekness.

There were large gardens at the back of the house and garages which had previously been stables. The garden, though neat and tidy, did not suit my father. He soon started corresponding with garden experts, the Bill Sowerbutts and Alan Gemmels of his day and with their help replanned the front garden. Rockeries filled with alpine plants took the place of a more conventional border. Beautiful flowering shrubs were planted in other borders. The young man who carried out this work was rather an unsavoury character. He used to boast to Sadie and me about his criminal exploits. He rode a motorbike recklessly and said he'd served an eighteen months' prison sentence for manslaughter, when he'd killed a pedestrian. We never knew how much of what he told us was invented.

When additional furniture was being bought for the house in Northumberland Street, what we had being inadequate, my father acquired an enormous bookcase. One day a large consignment of books arrived. I think he must have bought up someone's library. I now became an avid reader. Some of the books were beyond my comprehension, and I was so anxious to know how they ended that I virtually proof-read them, a habit I've found very difficult to break since. I remember being frightened by Edgar Allen Poe's 'The Raven' and mystified by Anna Karenina's behaviour. To give up everything for a man! I was about twelve at the time. I often escaped from my allotted household tasks on the pretext of doing my homework, with one of the books hidden inside a school textbook in case someone came in unexpectedly.

My brother was not very strong and was often off school with childish ailments. One of my father's customers was a governor of a small private school, Vernon House, situated on the Cliff. His own children attended this school, and he suggested that Sydney might benefit from being in a smaller group where he'd be less liable to infection. Sydney spent some happy years there and later transferred to Salford Grammar School, then on the Crescent.

While he was at Vernon House, the council announced that, as an economy measure, they were closing down Summer Hill School. The original intention had been to train girls who intended to become teachers, but few were following on to Teacher Training Colleges. They said that the girls who were leaving would have to sit a qualifying examination if they wished to go to Pendleton High School or Broughton High School. Mr. Allison, my father's customer, who then had a daughter at Summer Hill, and some other parents, resisted this stipulation. They said we should be allowed to transfer

Broughton High School

to the school of our choice – we had already passed the 11 plus. They were successful in their campaign, and so it was that Sadie and I changed over to Broughton High School. Many of the pupils were fee-paying and there were frequent clashes between the scholarship girls and the 'snobs'.

My father had, for some years, been interested in cars. When we lived in Great Cheetham Street, he had bought a succession of vehicles in varying stages of decrepitude. One was a grey Fiat with a dicky seat. Another car I remember was a yellow Belsize, which, parked outside our house, invited the jibes of ill-natured youth – yellow cab was then a euphemism for transport to a lunatic asylum. Father must have learned to drive by studying manuals. He never had a driving lesson. In those days it was not necessary to face the rigours of a driving test. The number of vehicles on the road was only a fraction of those running today. This raised the chances of survival for pedestrians, exposed to people in charge of lethal weapons over which they had little control. I remember one incident when an unwary girl dashed out of a side street on Leicester Road, right into the path of the car. Fortunately my father had mastered the emergency stop! The girl was helped off the bonnet of the car and escorted home, where she seemed to recover quickly from tis devastating experience.

Frederick: my father

Sometimes on Sundays we used to go on excursions to the countryside. Sydney and my father sat in the front, while Flo, Sadie and I squeezed into the back. Sadie and I often argued and occasionally exchanged blows. Flo, who sat sandwiched between us, seemed to get very disagreeable on these outings. We used to stop now and again to explore or pick wild flowers which grew more profusely in those days. Often we bought bunches of garden flowers which were trustingly displayed for sale on tables outside old-world cottages. They were usually 6d. or at most 1/-. a bunch. One selected one's flowers and left the money on the table. Then for the real treat! Tea in one of the cottages! New-laid eggs, home-made bread and cakes, jam and a pot of tea for 1/6d. Much as we enjoyed these outings, they were never free of incident. There was always some mishap to the decrepit car. Punctures were a recurrent disaster, due to venturing forth with balding tyres. We seemed to spend hours searching for garages where repairs were carried out and punctures laboriously mended. The terrain was at first Cheshire, or sometimes Derbyshire. Later, the spirit of adventure aroused, we embarked on more ambitious excursions to Wales and the Lake District.

In Great Cheetham Street the car had been parked outside the front door. Now my father had to reverse it down the drive of the house in Northumberland Street. The first time he attempted to do this, we were off to buy food for Sunday lunch at a nearby delicatessen, named the Titanic, because the owner was a survivor of that ill-fated vessel. An hour and a half later, he was still in the drive after dozens of forward and backward sorties. Somehow he could not synchronise the movements of the steering wheel with the car wheels. At last, somewhat bruised, the car was thriumphantly manoeuvred out of the drive.

One day we received a letter from Aunt Ray, who lived in South Africa to say that she was coming to England with her daughter, Adelaide, and asking if they could stay with us. Adelaide, still in her teens, was a budding pianist. She had given recitals in Cape Town and won a piano-playing competition there. Ray hoped she might further her career in England. There was soon friction between Flo and Ray, the latter being quick-tempered, but Flo had to restrain herself. Ray was addicted to garlic, which she regarded as a cure-all and the house reeked of it during her stay. It was many years before I could accept it as a culinary aid. Sadie and I were dazzled by Adie. Although extremely attractive and talented, she was completely unspoiled. Sometimes she slept with us in our double bed and talked to us till the early hours. She had lovely clothes to wear for her auditions and she used to let us try them on. She soon acquired a boy-friend in Manchester, a wholesale tobbaconist, who wined and dined her and proposed to her. But she made it clear that her music came first. She made some records and played on the radio. Later she performed at some concerts in London, but there she was, a small fish in a big pond and she and Ray soon returned to South Africa, where she had some success.

Aunt Flo, like the fisherman's wife in the fairy tale, was never satisfied. Having a larger house meant too much housework, although grandma did the cooking and other tasks and Sadie and I helped when coerced. Now she demanded a maid, and, unheard of in those days, a wage for her own services. This was little enough and reluctantly given, because my father knew she was already helping herself out of the housekeeping money. She kept a cashbox in her bedroom, which was full of half-crowns, which she counted with grim satisfaction from time to time, before depositing it in the Savings Bank. She had a sweet tooth and kept tins of Sovereign Devon Cream and treacle toffee in her room. The toffee was in slabs, and she had a small brass hammer with which she used to break it into manageable pieces. If we behaved, we were treated to pieces of toffee and, on the rare occasions when things were going exceptionally well, we were allowed to wield the hammer ourselves. Then the pieces were substantially larger.

Aunt Flo and grandma used to have morning tea in their bedroom. They had a gas fire fitted and a small gas ring. The tray was daintily set, the little jug of evaporated milk covered with a lace-trimmed mat weighted with coloured beads. Aunt Flo seemed to think this was the height of gentility.

Uncle Benny, my father's brother, was a frequent visitor to our house in Northumberland Street. Like the Old Testament gentleman of the same name he was the youngest member of the family and spoilt. He was very fond of the ladies and, although married, had a reputation as a philanderer. He used to go dancing and sometimes he would practise some of the intricate steps with me. At that time he did not have his own business and was often hard up, and once my father asked him if he would like to decorate our kitchen to earn some money. He agreed to do so and was given £5 to buy materials. We did not see Benny for a week or two. He had spent the money. Eventually the job was done by a painter and decorator. Once or twice I noticed Benny and my father muttering together in a quiet corner, and after one of his visits I found a note on the floor which read, 'Meet the birds at 7.30 p.m.'. Puzzled, I gave the note to granny. She and Flo must have kept a watching brief on father after that because, a week or so later, Flo said to Sadie and me, 'Don't kiss your father when he comes home tonight. He's been out with women!' I looked at him curiously when he came home from 'work', but he seemed his usual self.

Benny later went to live with one of his dancing partners, Gladys. She was a dark, doe-eyed woman, completely different from the shrewish Hetty, whom he left with his three children to care for. I don't know how, or if, he discharged his financial obligations to them, as he and Gladys proved to be prolific partners and eventually had six children. They escaped the wrath of Hetty by moving to a part of the country immortalised by the antics of Robin Hood. In Nottingham Benny built up a prosperous business, and Gladys, a convert to Judaism, became more zealous than any born Jew. They were pillars of the local synagogue. Even the budgerigar was indoctrinated and came out with phrases like, 'Joey is a nice clean boy for Shabbas'. Gladys was quite upset when two of their children 'married out' and found non-Jewish partners. Poor Hetty dedicated the rest of her life trying to find the whereabouts of her recalcitrant spouse and his 'whore', but they covered up their tracks too well, and she died a bitter woman.

4. Bronwen's Baby

Bronwen, the maid, joined the family. She was a Welsh girl, driven by unemployment in the valleys, and the unwelcome attentions of her stepfather, to seek work in England. Poorly equipped, there was nothing for her and her sisters but domestic service, wherever they could get it. In the mornings she wore a saxe-blue uniform and in the afternoons a black dress and dainty white cap and broderie Anglaise apron. How I envied her the pretty apron! Bronwen was nineteen or twenty, about six years older than me. She was a lively girl, fresh-complexioned and well-proportioned. Her voice had an attractive lilt. We had an unruly mongrel, Jip, which she quickly subdued, beating him cruelly, I thought, when he misbehaved, but he fawned round her and ignored us. On one occasion, when he was pursuing a bitch round the garden, she cooled his ardour by dousing him with a bucket of cold water.

Aunt Flo's behaviour towards her vacillated between fond embraces – which I then found puzzling – and scoldings and complaints about her work. I noticed how my father's eyes lit up when she was around. I regarded him as an old man then, though he must have been barely forty. I became Bronwen's confidante. She used to take me to the local cinema on Saturday afternoons, buying me sweets and chocolates. During the interval, she would tell me about her latest conquests, some met during walks in Heaton Park with her sister, also a maid in Higher Broughton, on their days off.

We had two garages behind the house, and as only one was used, my father let the other one to a man who had a business in the vicinity. He was a handsome, husky man. Bronwen was assiduous in opening the garage door for him each night and then locking it when he left. I used to think it was very thoughtful of her to go to all this trouble. Sometimes it seemed to take rather a long time, and she came back looking red and flustered. But Mr. Logan, the gentleman concerned, seemed very appreciative of her help. He gave her presents from time to time, and a lovely pair of fur-backed gloves for Christmas.

Bronwen's bedroom was next to the little wash-room which we all used at night, unless we had a bath in the bathroom. My father seemed to have his ablutions later and later at night until we no longer heard him go to bed. One night he walked into her room and her welcoming arms.

There were ructions when Bronwen was discovered to be pregnant. In the circumstances, either she had to go, or Grandma and Aunt Flo. Bronwen stayed! It was rumoured that the baby could be Mr. Logan's, but father seemed quite happy with his live-in mistress.

My father was not a religious man. In his later years, he leaned to agnosticism rather than the avowed atheism of his younger days. When Granny and Aunt Flo were in charge of the household, the Jewish festivals, such as the Day of Atonement, the Jewish New Year and the Passover, were always observed. Granny lit the candles every Friday night. With a graceful movement of hands and a gentle benediction, she welcomed in the Sabbath. A special chicken meal was invariably served. But what often puzzled me is why, when Granny and Aunt Flo departed, leaving Bronwen mistress of the house, he decided that Passover, the festival to commemorate the flight of the Jews from Egypt, should be celebrated in the traditional manner.

The Haggadah, an illustrated booklet derived from the Talmud, gives explicit details on how to prepare for the Passover.

The House must be cleaned and the kitchen cleared of everything used during the rest of the year. Cutlery and crockery and cooking utensils kept specifically for the Passover are brought out of hiding. All food must be disposed of, bread especially is taboo. Foods to be eaten during the festival must be sanctioned by a monitoring body, the Beth Din. These approved foods are sold at exorbitant prices in the Jewish shops. The offerings in the bakers are irresistible – delicious sweetmeats, cakes and different kinds of matzos. Whether Bronwen bothered to observe the rites as far as the preparation of the household was concerned, I don't know. But there we sat, in the draughty drawing room on Séder night, the first and most significant night of Pésach, my father at one end of the table, Bronwen, big with child, at the other. The candles sputtered and molten wax dribbled down the stem of the silver candelabra.

Everything on the table was symbolic of the exodus: matzos, unleavened bread, signifying the haste with which the Jews left Egypt; kosher wine, bitter herbs and horseradish to convey the bitterness of the lives of their ancestors as slaves; the shank bone of a lamb, to commemorate the sacrifice of the Paschal Lamb when God punished the Egyptians and saved the Israelites. We each had our

Haggadah, telling the story of the flight from Egypt and the vengeance wreaked on the Egyptians by God, beginning with the death of the first-born and the subsequent plagues. Then follows a glorification of God At a certain point in the ceremony, the participants are advised to break off for supper.

Sydney and my father read the service, which involves role-playing, the son asking the questions and the father supplying the answers. During the ritual, wine was repeatedly sipped, and Sadie and I grew quite excited, and, unsupervised, drank more than we should of the sweet, red wine. I felt my face getting hotter and hotter. Itchy spots came up on my arms. We kept giggling and my father became angry. One of the candles went out. I picked up a box of matches and relit it. Unthinkingly, I put the unspent match back in the box. It exploded. So did my father!

The Haggadah concludes with a story redolent of the folk lore that is part of the heritage of people the world over, building up in repetitive style to this crescendo:

> Then the angel of death came and slew
> the slaughterer, who had slaughtered
> the ox, which had drunk the water, which
> had extinguished the fire, which burnt
> the stick, which had beaten the dog, which
> had bitten the cat, which had devoured the
> kid, which my father bought for two zuzim;
> only one kid, only one kid.

Grandma and Flo had moved to a flat on The Cliff. Sadie, Sydney and I visited them regularly. Eventually, when Grandma became ill, father began to visit them. Their flat was one of several in a large house. Aunt Flo became friendly with the bachelor inmate of another flat, a Mr. Barrett. A subtle change took place in Aunt Flo. No-one could pretend that a butterfly had emerged from that ungainly, angular form, but she certainly began to dress more stylishly and take on an almost feminine look. She even used cosmetics sparingly. It seemed obvious that she and Mr. Barrett were more than just good friends, and Grandma told us that things were going on between them that she didn't approve of!

Granny used to like to read the spicy bits in the newspapers, and as her hand shook when she used her magnifying glass, we used to read to her on our visits.

Meanwhile, Bronwen was being read to from "The Decameron" by my father, she informed me. I had discovered this book in his collection and had read it some time before. I wasn't pleased to hear that she was being regaled with its bawdy contents as an aphrodisiac. In fact, I was becoming more and more disenchanted with the situation. Although we lived in a neighbourhood where there was little casual contact between neighbours, remarks were sometimes made to Sadie and me by unkind people that made us uncomfortable.

When Bronwen's time drew near, she left the house to be looked after until she had the baby. My father once discussed the situation with us. He said he had thought seriously about marrying her. He was very fond of her and she of him. But he didn't think it would prove to be a lasting relationship. And the disparity in age might cause problems later. I think he was right.

My father then installed a housekeeper to look after us. She was the first of many. She was an amiable, untidy Irish woman, by the name of Maggie. One day, we were sitting in the kitchen having our dinner, when there was an impatient knocking at the door. When we opened it, we found an irate woman standing there, holding a baby in a shawl in her arms. She was almost hysterical. She said that she'd told Mr. Leach that she couldn't look after this baby any longer and he must find someone else to do so. She dumped the baby – our half-brother – into the arms of the outraged Maggie. She gave the baby to Sadie to hold and immediately rang up father and told him what had happened. He arrived home very quickly and Maggie gave him a piece of her mind and said it was disgraceful for girls of our age to be subjected to such a thing. That was the only time we saw the baby. Father took him away to another child-minder and he was soon adopted by someone in Wales.

Maggie, Sydney and Hilda

Bronwen found work with a family near the Half-Way House, after arrangements had been made for the baby's future. She rang me up one day and called round to have a chat. She was wearing a 'gold' chain with red stones, a present from an admirer. I told her I thought it was lovely and she immediately took it off and put it round my neck. She took me to see her new place of work and I was pleased to find that she had a very pleasant family to work for. I never saw her again.

5. Surrogate Mothers

Maggie was a kind woman, but an incompetent housekeeper. We soon discovered she drank heavily. Often she returned from her evenings off much the worse for drink. Sometimes father came home late, and we used to barricade ourselves in our bedroom when we heard her ranting and raving after one of her convivial evenings. Next day she was always apologetic and contrite. But one day she overstepped the mark.

My father had ordered some bottles of wine from the local wine merchant. Maggie had been unable to resist temptation and was paralytic when we got home from school. She lay in a drunken stupor for a couple of days. Her sister, who was in service in Manchester, was sent for, and she told us that Maggie was an alcoholic and couldn't hold a job down. She treacherously offered to take Maggie's place, but she was told to take Maggie away.

The next applicant for the job of housekeeper was a woman with a husband and small daughter. He worked away during the week and only made his appearance at weekend. She was a small, plump woman – he was a dark hirsute man. They had the cloak-room, a reasonably-sized room, as their private sitting room. She saw her daughter, a little scrawny child, as a future Pavlova and made her practice her ballet steps assiduously. Dressed in her tutu, she looked most unprepossessing, like an undernourished chicken. Sydney, at that time, was an attractive and gentle child. I sensed her feeling of resentment towards him. I noticed at meal times she always gave him smaller portions of food than her daughter and I once remonstrated with her, but she was quite unpleasant and I was rather afraid of her. It soon became obvious that, when her husband was away, she was flaunting her wares for my father's benefit.

One night I woke up in a cold sweat. Since Grandma and Aunt Flo had left, Sadie and I slept in the front bedroom. I thought I could hear movements in my father's room. I was distrustful of him since his affair with Bronwen, and felt sure that he and the housekeeper were misbehaving. I hurried into my father's room. But there he was, alone, snoring away. I dashed back to bed shivering, wondering what would have happened if my suspicions had proven to be correct. I was relieved when they left, having found a house of their own.

I was going through a hypochondriacal stage at this time. Medical books I browsed through confirmed my worst suspicions. I was a walking miracle! Host to every disease known to man! During Aunt Flo's reign, I had once told her that I was sure I had cancer and I reeled off the symptoms. That night, alarmed, she took me to the doctor. I was annoyed that she was not explicit enough in her conversation with the doctor and refrained from using the dreaded word. But she made it clear that she thought I might be seriously ill. The doctor gave me a cursory examination and then turned to Flo. 'My dear, you need some help!' she said. 'You look far from well!' We went home, Flo, looking bewildered, clutching a large bottle the doctor had prescribed for her.

My father was not very helpful when I wished to discuss the state of my health with him. One night I informed him that I was sure I had diabetes. I used to eat far more sweets and chocolates than was good for me and thought I might have reaped an expected harvest. 'What makes you think you've got diabetes?' he asked – seriously, I thought. I told him that I had to keep passing water. 'My God!' he exclaimed. 'I must have it too!'

How I laughed when I read Jerome K. Jerome's books some time later and identified with the hypochondriacal George. I think it was in 'Three Men in a Boat', though I also read 'The Idle Thoughts of an Idle Fellow' and 'Three Men on the Bummel'. I wonder if they'd survive the test of time if I re-read them now!

It soon became apparent that some of the women who applied for the post of housekeeper to widowers hoped to become mistress of the house if they played their cards right. I'm sure they quickly abandoned the idea when they found themselves ensconced in our house. Two adolescent girls, and a boy who used the kitchen as a laboratory and was always carrying out smelly experiments, were a bit too much to put up with. My father's helpless air seemed to appeal to women's mothering instincts. He often ate on his own at night and was waited on hand and foot. He even seemed incapable of pouring out a cup of tea for himself.

Sadie and I took it upon ourselves to see that the coal scuttle was full at night so that he need not go down the cellar for coal. His endearing smile and affectionate manner seemed adequate compensation. I often called for him after I had done my homework, to escort him home from work and carry his attache case. This often contained important objects like bags of sweets – I never knew him to be without a supply.

Father went to work later and later with the passing of the years, until, eventually before he retired, his only customers were people on the way home from work. While he was in bed, the people who worked for him got up to various tricks. At one period, money kept disappearing and eventually the culprit, a book-keeper, was caught red-handed. My father, who had a puckish sense of humour, was tickled by his dramatically uttered words, 'I don't know what made me do it!' and repeated this phrase ad nauseam.

There was also a cutter, addicted to drink. When he was sober, his work was perfect, but quite often garments had to be altered because they had been cut when he was under the influence. He also had an unpleasant habit of taking on the role of collector for goods supplied and pocketing the money. Eventually, of course, he had to go.

Sydney was taking private lessons in Hebrew in preparation for his barmitzvah. A young man came to the house once a week, and the lessons were conducted in the cloak-room. This man had blue eyes and ginger hair and beard. There was a song popular at that time – 'She's got eyes of blue, I never cared for eyes of blue, but she's got eyes of blue, that's my weakness now'. Sadie and I were a mischievous pair and, when the lessons were in progress, we used to sing through the keyhole of the adjoining room, 'He's got eyes of blue'. Not satisfied with this, we added another stanza – 'He's got a little ginger beard, I never cared for little ginger beards'. The young man wisely didn't react – perhaps he needed the money – but Sydney told my father and we got a good ticking off.

In the Manchester area there was then a flourishing chain of sweet shops Meesons – the poor man's Thorntons. A sign in the window proclaimed 'Buy a quarter and for another 1d get another quarter'. My father often sent me to the branch in Market Street to get ½ lb. of sweets, and we used to demolish them between us. No wonder I was plagued with acne in my teens! Once when I went there to buy the usual sweets I noticed a prosperous-looking man buying Easter novelities. He looked at me looking at him and said, 'Choose whatever you like, dear!' I demurred, but he insisted, and I chose an Easter egg. I got a lecture when I produced my gift on my return to father's offices in Fountain Street, and was told I must never, under any circumstances, take anything from strange men.

Our house was in Northumberland Street and the name, Melrose House, was inscribed, with the number – 35 – on the pillars leading to the drive. One day a workman arrived with some gold leaf, which he carried carefully between some sheets of paper. He irradiated the number and letters by pressing the gold leaf firmly onto them. They shone vividly afterwards. We lived near the top end of the street which led onto Leicester Road. The bottom end came out onto Bury New Road.

When we went to town, we invariably walked to Leicester Road and waited for the tram. It was not a good service then, and the bus service since has scarcely improved. Eventually the tram would clatter up. I usually sat downstairs. Two long, slatted benches ran the whole length of the tram and you sat facing the passengers on the opposite row. I used to study them intently. Sometimes you found your gaze locked in someone else's and played at staring them out. It meant defeat to drop one's eyes first.

For some time I found it hard to accept my mother's untimely death. She had been suddenly snatched away from us. We children had returned from school on that fateful day to be told that she'd died in hospital. But we'd never seen her dead, nor did we attend the funeral.

I used to fantasise that she might still be alive. Maybe she'd run off with another man. There had sometimes been stormy rows between my mother and father. And so I was particularly interested in women passengers who seemed to be about my mother's age and who, by a stretch of imagination, bore some resemblance to her. I was very near-sighted and didn't wear glasses! But my stare never evoked any response and I had to come to terms with her death.

The tram proceeded on its noisy way down Great Cheetham Street, past the Empire Cinema where I had spent many happy hours with Bronwen, and then turned left at Bury New Road. On the right-hand corner of Bury New Road stood the Rialto, a fine art deco building. Now it's a tawdry bingo hall. The tram conductor wore a peaked hat and carried a ticket machine. From an interesting array of coloured tickets he selected the appropriate one and punched it with a machine. This action produced a satisfying ping. Toy tram-conductor sets, complete with peaked hats, enlivened many a small boy's Christmas in those days. My brother had one. Bury New Road was then a thriving Jewish area, with its many shops, bakers, delicatessens, grocers, trimming shops and small factories. One ignored the sinister Strangeways prison, which loomed darkly as one approached town. The Jews, one-time immigrants, moved later into Higher Broughton and Prestwich and beyond, and now Asians have taken over the area and given it their particular flavour. The tram eventually wended its way up Market Street, where I usually alighted near Lewis's.

Father often took us to the cinema on Saturday night, usually to the second house film. The cinema was in its heyday then. Sometimes when we lived in Great Cheetham Street, we went to the Marlborough, just round the corner in St. James's Road. One night we were sitting there, enjoying the film, "The Scarlet Letter", starring Lillian Gish, when my father nudged me urgently and whispered, "Get up quietly, we're going!" The message was relayed to Sadie and Sydney, who were as reluctant as I was to go. Outside father announced that he'd had a sudden premonition that the cinema was going to burn down. Our annoyance gave way to excitement. We rushed round early next morning – not my father, who was not an early riser – expecting to see it razed to the ground, but no, there it stood, completely unscathed. It occurred to me later that father may have been bored with the film!

There was a croft a bit further along St. James's Road, which housed a very unprepossessing cinema, aptly named the Bug Hut, but I remember going there only once.

There were periods when we went to Broughton High School when we were without housekeepers. Sadie and I didn't have dinners at school. The Jewish girls who lived too far away to go home took sandwiches, as they were usually from orthodox families. We certainly weren't, but it would have offended them if we'd partaken of the school dinners provided for the rest of the girls. And we didn't want sandwiches. So sometimes we had to buy food from the shops on Bury New Road during the dinner hour and hastily prepare some lunch at home. Tempers were somewhat frayed and we used to quarrel. Sadie usually assumed the role of cook and I did the menial tasks. Once, when she was particularly bossy, I hit her on the head with a frying pan I was washing. I was immediately struck with fear and remorse, in that order – an image of myself on a murder charge flashed through my mind, and I was unusually submissive and solicitous towards her for the rest of the day. Fortunately, these bleak periods did not occur very often, because, with high unemployment, there was usually someone available to take on the onerous role of housekeeper.

I was quite a good scholar and matriculated when I was sixteen. It was never even considered that I might go to University. That was usually the preserve of men at that time. Also, I thought that I might leave school at seventeen and do a year as a student teacher, for which a small pittance was paid, and then go to Training College. My father favoured that.

Sadie was not interested in school work and made little effort. She was ready to leave at sixteen. She was often in scrapes and I felt embarrassed by her lapses of behaviour. On one occasion, she nearly forfeited the right to attend a Christmas party by acquiring five misconduct marks and, along with other miscreants, was hauled out during a school assembly to have the weighty matter discussed. Their heinous crimes included misdeeds like not wearing gloves to and from school, eating in the street wearing school uniform, talking in class. The headmistress magnanimously decided to allow them the privilege of attending the party if they made a big effort to conform to school rules in future. However, Sadie had the Lichtenstein flair for music and was doing very well at the piano. In spite of her poor performance at school, she had a very successful business career later in life as a shipping agent, with a travel agency as a sideline.

We still continued to visit Bobby. Jane, when she was nearing forty, married a widower. He died a year or two later. She very quickly acquired a second husband, which seemed to make up for her slow start in the matrimonial stakes.

Mark had died of lung cancer a few years earlier. His was a lonely and unfulfilled life. The girl he would have liked to marry was a Christian and was not accepted by the family. However, another uncle, Lionel, did marry out. He was his own man and was not going to be dictated to by family prejudices. When Jane married her widower, Lionel and his wife moved in. What a transformation took place in that dingy little house. It became a clean, comfortable home. Bobby respected Doris and they lived amicably together until she and Lionel found a flat in the Broughton Park area. It was a very happy marriage and Lionel was disconsolate when she died some years later.

Granny died at the age of 83 after suffering a stroke. Flo then moved to a room in Great Cheetham Street near Mandley Park. Occasionally she visited us, but we usually went to see her. Her movements were restricted as she suffered from arthritis. At that time Salford council had started an experiment of setting up a few homes for about twelve elderly people who didn't need nursing care and whom they didn't want to institutionalise. They were sometimes ex-professional people with no families. My father saw our family doctor and he managed to secure a place for Flo in one of these homes in Bury New Road. It appeared to be a satisfactory solution to her problem. But Flo seemed to antagonise people and, quite soon, she was transferred to the geriatric section of Hope Hospital.

It was saddening to visit her there. To avoid the grasping hands and pleading eyes of the old ladies who never had any visitors. To smell the suffocating odour of incontinence. When she died, it was a release for her and a relief for those who knew her.

6. Wolf at the Door

As a credit tailor in the '30s, my father was often in the situation where clients could not pay for goods they had obtained. Sometimes father worked a kind of barter system. He had a set of dentures made by a poor dentist in exchange for a suit the dentist had had made to measure and couldn't pay for. Small wonder the dentist was unsuccessful. The dentures he made were useless – father could only eat with them out! They were usually stuffed in his overcoat pocket in a paper bag.

One night I was foraging in his overcoat pocket in the unlit hall for some toffee and tried to break a piece of what I thought was a slab of Devon cream toffee. It resisted my attempts, and proved, to my horror, on closer inspection, to be his upper plate!

On another occasion, I remember the defaulter was an impecunious headmaster. He had a wife who was an excellent dressmaker, and she undertook to give my sister a course in dressmaking as a form of barter for unpaid debts. My sister eventually made a dress for herself and me and, as far as I know, has never sewn anything since.

It so happened that the headmaster was taking his top class on a camping holiday in Derbyshire, and my sister, brother and myself were invited to go with them, free of charge, to settle the account. He had a feckless daughter, a few years older than Sadie and me, who was supposed to be keeping an eye on us. The boys were a tough lot, and Sydney was like a fish out of water. He stayed with us. The headmaster had brought along two youths who worked in the kitchen. They told Sadie and me that they were professional footballers and were just helping out. Twice a week they went to Manchester to sign on with their teams, they said. We discovered later that they were on the dole and were signing on at their local labour exchange.

The headmaster was kept busy with his charges; we declined to accompany them on their excursions. His daughter quickly found a boy friend in the village and spent most of her time in his cottage. We were left to our own devices. The youths, when they had discharged their duties, pursued Sadie and me. We rebuffed their amorous advances and managed to keep them at bay, but Sydney was disturbed by their antics. He was also bored with his role of gooseberry. He rang home and told my father about the goings on at the camp and said he wanted to go home.

Our housekeeper, Mrs. Chester, a rather grim, humourless woman, arrived next day to take us all back home. We packed up and left. She sat with pursed lips on the journey back, no doubt thinking we'd encouraged the lads, and wondering whether there would be any repercussions from the frolics. I felt her enquiring eyes travelling from Sadie to me, as I sat with eyes cast down, emitting an occasional sigh, enjoying the role of an unhappy heroine.

Being next to the youngest in his family, my father felt overshadowed by his formidable brothers and sisters. He said they bullied him. Benny, the youngest, was spoiled, and anyway he asserted his ego in polygamy. My father found an outlet in conversation which developed more and more into a monologue with the passing years. Whoever coined the phrase, "They must have been vaccinated with a gramophone needle," must have had him in mind. Later in life he called the television the curse of civilisation. He resented the straying eyes when he tried to compete with its more hypnotic charms.

He had socialist convictions and corresponded with Labour politicians and M.P.s, advising them on what policies they should pursue. He wrote to the local Labour M.P., Konni Zilliacus, for some years – they were on first-name terms. He was very concerned about the growth of so-called national socialism in Germany and the emergency of Hitler with his doctrine of anti-semitism. We had relatives in Berlin and their letters were full of grim foreboding.

Along with thousands of small business men here, my father was suffering from the effects of the slump. People could no longer afford more expensive made-to-measure clothes. They were buying off-the-peg ready-to-wear suits and clothes. Since the departure of Granny and Aunt Flo, Sadie and I had been in the habit of buying our clothes from Philips' warehouse in Church Street, Manchester, where he had an account. Whenever we needed any new clothes, we just mentioned it and he told us to go and choose whatever we wanted. He was very indulgent and never refused us anything. It came as a shock one day when we asked if we could get new dresses and he said no, he couldn't afford it. Only then did I realise how bad things were.

From large premises in Fountain Street, he moved to a much smaller place in Mosley Street, opposite the Art Gallery. His business had dwindled to the extent that he had to dispose of his staff, a book-keeper, shorthand typist, sales representative and debt collector and cutter. An old tailoress used to come and sew for him at night. There was only a small waiting room and a large office-cum-work-room. To get to the toilet you had to walk through the adjoining cloth warehouse, which was rat-infested. People used to go to the toilet in twos. My father would use a bucket when he was alone. Sadie worked for him for a time as a typist and general dogsbody, but as soon as she could she found another job in Whitworth Street.

Because of his unsocial hours, my father didn't get to work till about four o'clock, and he took food for himself and the old lady. He told a tale with great glee about how once she picked up the wrong bag. It contained his discarded fish bones and tomato skin, and when he looked at her, she was eating his remains. He hadn't the heart to tell her, but salved his conscience by giving her a nice piece of cake.

His propensity for letter-writing not only found a political outlet. For some time he had been writing to a lady who had gone to Australia with her mother, in the wake of her two brothers who had emigrated there the previous year. She had known my father's family in Manchester and had been quite friendly with Flo and had written to her occasionally from Melbourne. When Flo departed, my father began to write to Cicily. Or it may have been the other way round. He hid her letters on the top shelf of the sitting room cupboards. But I'd seen them arrive in the post and tracked them down and used to read them when I was alone in the house. The letters were fluent and interesting and told about her life in Melbourne where she'd opened a shop selling woollen garments.

One letter interested me. He must have told her about Bronwyn because she asked why he hadn't married the girl. I don't know what his reply was, but obviously Cicily's scruples were overcome as the correspondence continued. Her mother had died some months before and she was feeling rather homesick and missing her many friends in the Manchester area. One day my father said she was coming on a visit to Manchester and he hinted that there was a possibility of their marrying. I don't know whether he apprised her of the state of his business and I wondered then and since what induced her to take such a risk when things were going so well for her there.

I must admit to a feeling of relief at the prospect of someone taking father off our hands. I had a strong feeling that he was going to become something of a liability with advancing age and eccentricity. Cissie, as we soon began to call her, was thirty-seven when she came to Manchester. Several well-meaning friends warned her of the risks she was taking – a widower with three children – two of them adolescent girls. But father's winsome charm and helpless air must have appealed to her mothering instincts, and she decided to marry him, even though it included these three offspring.

I had met Cissie once or twice before she went to Australia, but I did not know her very well. I was charmed by her when she came to visit us on her return to Manchester. I am not implying that disenchantment set in later, but of course, in life, halcyon days are transient. She was of ample proportions, had rosy cheeks and the attractive appealing eyes of the myopic, hidden behind thick glasses. She exuded vitality and good health. Blessed with a sense of humour, she brought fun and laughter into our house. She seemed to me like an older sister. Sadie did not feel the same rapport with her, but Sydney, who got on with everybody, accepted her.

Cissie

Cissie began to add feminine touches to our rather austere household. Attractive table linen began to appear, and the best china and cutlery were taken from cupboards and drawers and used. Many of her own possessions and books were mingled with ours. I particularly enjoyed Mary Webb's "Precious Bane" and "Gone to Earth". She brought linen sheets with her, a family heirloom. I really envied her these and used to finger them appreciatively when I saw them in the airing cupboard and wished I could have them on my bed. She enjoyed the role of hostess, and we often entertained and went visiting. Many of her friends were teachers. She herself had been a secretary in a Manchester factory.

Occasionally a chink appeared in the armour of content. Once Cissie was very angry when she brought a cake out of the sideboard and found that someone had picked off most of the cherries and nuts that decorated the top. The culprit proved to be Sydney. I couldn't see what all the fuss was about. That kind of thing had been normal behaviour before she wielded her civilising influence. Then it had been a case of who got there first. Also, Sydney was always seized with a desire to go to the lavatory immediately a meal was put out for him (I don't think it was the sight of the food, Cissie being a good cook) and this really exasperated her.

Prior to the advent of Cissie, I had embarked on a course of student teaching. I worked in a senior girls' school in Leicester Road, and as far as I remember I was there four days a week and one day at Broughton High School. Part of my time was spent in observation and the rest in working with backward readers and occasionally with a class. I was quite happy there and found the staff very helpful. One of my best friends, a daughter of the man who had been responsible for Sydney going to Vernon House, was also doing a practice at Leicester Road.

There was a fly in the ointment, unfortunately. The headmistress was an unpleasant character with whom my father had crossed swords when I was at Summer Hill School on Eccles Old Road. She was then geography mistress. She had favourites and girls whom she victimised in every class. I fell into the latter category. Most of the girls could cope with her unpleasantness, but I was very sensitive and started feigning illness rather than go to school on the days when she took geography with my class. Even my self-centred father realised all was not well and finally visited the school. He saw the headmistress and Miss Sweeney, the lady in question. After that she was sickly sweet to me. Now I felt like a snared rabbit. She veiled any animosity towards me but did her best to undermine my confidence, already sadly lacking. I knew with certainty that I wouldn't get into college. She had to send a confidential report on my capabilities.

And then came the day when the local H.M.I. (school inspector) sat in at a lesson. I chose to do arithmetic, teaching what was called the unity method. If three men plough a field in seven days, how long will it take eight men? After working out several examples on the board with the class and then letting volunteers do part of the process on the board – children love playing the role of teacher – I set some down for them to work out themselves. There was quite a high success rate, and Mr. Parish, the H.M.I. for Salford, gave me a good report. Miss Sweeney was obviously displeased and expressed surprise. I later went to Leeds for an interview and was told that, though I hadn't got a place that year, I should re-apply the following year. But I decided against it. Now the priority seemed to be to earn some money. (I was to return to teaching more than twenty years later, when my eldest daughter started a course at a speech therapy college and my youngest commenced school.)

About this time I made the acquaintance of a young man by the name of Wolf. One of Cissie's friends was headmistress of a Jewish school in Salford. She rang up one day and said there was a student from Israel, then Palestine, staying with a friend of hers. He was studying at Salford Technical College on the Crescent. He needed help with his English and was willing to teach Hebrew in exchange. Vera, Cissie's friend, wondered whether I might be interested. She thought it would also be an opportunity for him to make friends with an English girl. His credentials seemed to be all right. His father was Medical Officer in Tel Aviv. I said I would meet him and decide.

Wolf turned up one day at an arranged time. He was quite a handsome youth with black hair, an aquiline nose and dark, impudent eyes. Cissie produced afternoon tea, and we all got acquainted. His English was good enough for us to understand each other. Then Cissie withdrew and left us together in the drawing room. I was wearing carpet slippers, as it was a poorly-heated room and my feet were cold. No sooner had Cissie left the room than Wolf snatched off one of my slippers and proceeded to polish his shoes with it. I had a feeling that this did not augur well for language lessons.

In fact, he proved to be a wolf in sheep's clothing. Most of the lesson was spent in resisting his advances. I learned little Hebrew. I wasn't really interested, but I was quite conscientious in helping him with his English. I gave him exercises to take home and sometimes I set him essays.

He usually did his homework. One day he boasted that he could ad lib on any subject without preparation. He certainly possessed mental acuity to match his physical agility. Cissie was very prim and proper and if she had known what Wolf was really like, she'd have ordered him out of the house! Once he made a lunge at me as I moved over to the bookcase. I struggled to get away, but he held me tightly in his arms. Oh well, I thought, relaxing against him. We stood near the window, and there was Cissie, coming up the drive, looking straight at us, I thought. But she was very short-sighted and perhaps didn't see us. Anyway, nothing was said.

However, I had no illusions about Wolf's feelings towards me. To him I was just a sexual object, and I regarded him as an arrogant, but amusing male, who had to be kept in order. I experienced the first stirrings of feminism.

Wolf was an intellectual snob and was disgusted to hear that I intended to do a crash course in shorthand and typing. He thought I should pursue an academic career. When the summer term ended, he went back to Israel and I heard no more of him.

Cissie set about trying to inject some life into my father's business. She obtained clothes, mostly ladies' wear, on approval from warehouses off High Street that father had dealt with for a long time, and used to take them round to his customers, in the hope of getting some orders. With her pleasant personality, she was quite successful, but it was hard work trudging round with a heavy suitcase.

We had a woman who used to come in a few days a week to clean the house, but Cissie did the cooking. There was a standing joke that she always produced burnt offerings. One side of the cakes she made was invariably browner than the other. She always blamed the gas cooker, and said the gas jets were uneven. We began to notice that all was not brightness and light any longer.

She must have felt overwhelmed by the realisation that the situation she had walked into so lightheartedly was proving to be a trap. She was often unwilling to talk when she came back from one of her business trips. You might even say she sulked. Sadie kept well out of the way. She was enjoying a lively social life, going to Jewish clubs and dances. And I often went to friends' houses when I wasn't studying. Sydney used to hop over the back-garden wall and join his friends who lived in Broom Lane.

One summer's day when Cissie and I were at home alone, we had tea in the garden. She said, 'Hilda, I want to talk to you'. Warning bells rang in my head. She continued to tell me that a friend of hers had caught venereal disease from her husband. He'd had it before he married her and had received medical treatment and thought he was cured. However, his wife had contracted it, and it could only have been through him. She asked me what I thought the wife should do!

Poor Cissie! She'd chosen this oblique way of telling me what she could tell no-one else. I felt so sorry for her. But, I suppose, irrationally, I felt some resentment at having to share her burden. I just told her that, if the man in question really thought he was free of the disease and had unwittingly passed it on to her friend, she ought to forgive him. Cissie seemed to agree.

However, there were happy times too. Both Cissie and my father loved music. He was a competent pianist, although he claimed to have had only one term's tuition. He used to buy a music publication that came out at regular intervals. The contents often included excerpts from operas. We used to gather round the piano and sing while he played. Our rendition of arias such as 'On with the motley, the paint and the powder', one of our favourites, must have been awful, but we all fancied ourselves as undiscovered virtuosos.

The D'Oyley Carte Opera Company came to Manchester each year for a Gilbert and Sullivan season, and Cissie had gone regularly before she went to Australia. She now introduced us to some of their operas. We saw 'The Mikado', 'H.M.S. Pinafore' and 'The Pirates of Penzance'. We had an H.M.V. wind-up gramophone, a console model. If you didn't wind it up sufficiently, the lovely music wailed to an untimely end. We had a good collection of records, including some by Enrico Caruso, Nellie Melba and Clara Butt. Amongst the records was one made by my cousin, Adelaide Newman, when she was in England.

7. Salad Days in Derbyshire

Cissie was a keen walker and, for the first time, we experienced the delights of rambling in Derbyshire. Years before, her brothers had founded perhaps the first Manchester Rambling Club, along with other enthusiasts.

Our favourite area was Derbyshire. We often went to Chinley, Hayfield or Edale, Friends of Cissie and ours sometimes accompanied us. We walked from Castleton to Hope. When we called at farm houses for tea, the owners exclaimed in delight at seeing her after a long absence.

The most memorable experience we had was when she took us for a holiday to a unique Quaker vegetarian guest house, situated in a village called Crich, near Matlock. Her brothers had discovered this place in one of their rambles. The proprietors were a Mr. and Mrs. Ludlow. Close by was the Quaker village of Fritchley, where the host and hostess and some of the guests wended their way on Sundays to take part in the services at the Friends' Meeting House. Mrs. Ludlow often stood up and led the prayers at these gatherings, but the usually loquacious Mr. Ludlow rarely spoke, being content to pray silently like most of the congregation. Even unbelievers, drawn initially only by curiosity, admitted to a feeling of spiritual uplift after attending one of these services.

The people who stayed at "The Briars" were not all vegetarians. Some came for a change, others because of its position in the heart of Derbyshire and because the amenities offered were to their liking, orthodox Jews, that they might not offend against their dietary laws. At the other extreme were vegans, who rejected dairy products. They could sometimes be detected by nervous tics and twitchings, having contracted diseases of the nervous system through lack of essential nutrients in their diet. No forbidden odours ever wafted from the large kitchen when the food was being cooked.

Even the household cats were unwilling participants in this regime, though on occasions they were to be seen catching and consuming unwary birds, leaving barely a feather. Field mice, too, often fell victim to eager tooth and claw. The cats did not toy lazily with their mesmerised prey, as do well-fed carnivores, but ate them greedily,

"The Briars", Crich

down to the last whisker. The gentle Kate Ludlow turned away her head, when they laid their prey at her feet, offering her first choice.

At meal times families and friends were encouraged to sit not in their nuclear groups but at large tables, moving about and meeting different people. Serving dishes were brought to the table, and grace was said by Mr. and Mrs. Ludlow. Places at the head or foot of the table were adroitly avoided by the initiated, because it was here that one had to pour out tea or serve soup. Several minutes later, after serving dishes had been passed and returned to each guest, amid a forest of moving arms, the meal began.

The host, in his rich, fruity Charles Laughton voice, could be heard making conversation at his table. He took pride in his skill as a raconteur, and anyone foolish enough to interrupt him was the recipient of a glance of displeasure, doubly disconcerting because of Mr. Ludlow's bad squint. He ate with evident enjoyment. By contrast, his wife, who sat at another table, kept an attentive eye on the guests, spoke little and ate sparingly.

For breakfast there was usually porridge or cornflakes. There were mounds of milled nuts, sticky juicy raisins, bowls of fresh fruit, wholemeal bread, honey and marmalade. Eggs were either boiled or scrambled to a fluffy perfection. Lunch consisted of a vegetarian savoury and several vegetables, grown in the garden, followed by one of Mrs. Ludlow's delectable puddings. Afternoon tea, which was handed round by the young and able-bodied, would have been frowned on in these days of calorie counting, but the home-made scones and cakes were too delicious to resist. The evening meal, referred to as supper, was soup, salad, followed by cheese and biscuits, and the ubiquitous dandelion coffee. Small wonder that many guests complained that they had put on weight at the end of their stay at "The Briars".

Every morning after breakfast, the guests assembled outside the house and went on a conducted walk. On several of my visits – I went there quite often – a retired schoolmaster, over eighty years old, who knew the district well and was still a keen walker, led the walks. Though there was a sprinkling of young people and a few families, the guests tended to be middle-aged and included several octogenarians. I introduced some of my friends to "The Briars" and spent my honeymoon there some years later.

Frequently Mr. Ludlow took guests who had no cars on outings to places such as Matlock and Bakewell in his old Rolls Royce, which was his pride and joy. When he opened the bonnet, he carefully cleaned and polished the engine and mechanisms until they shone and gleamed. A stop was made for afternoon tea, and he always bought a picture postcard for Kate, which he stamped and posted. She received it next day, with exclamations of delight.

After the evening meal, when the staff had gone home, the guests cleared the tables, washed up and put away the cutlery and dishes. Then they went and relaxed in the comfortable lounge. Here a piano was the only means of entertainment and, as the small village cinema had closed through lack of support, the visitors could either converse with each other or amuse themselves. Games were played, and most people participated. To go and sit in the 'quiet' lounge meant an admission of decrepitude few were willing to make, and it was usually left to the old and infirm.

Eventually the Ludlows retired to a small country cottage nearby and the place was taken over by another Quaker couple with two young sons. They invested their life savings in what was, to them, primarily a business venture. Improvements had to be made if it was to become more efficient and show larger profits. "The Briars" lost its unique quality. It was no longer a retreat. It was merely another guest house.

8. Woman's Work

There were two commercial colleges in Manchester, both in Spring Gardens. One was Pitman's and the other Loreburn's. Pitman's had the better reputation. My father went along with me to see the principal. He said that once students became proficient, they were more or less assured of a job. Though they offered a range of subjects, I wanted to do only shorthand and typing, as matriculation was considered proof of academic ability. My father paid for one term's tuition and said he would see how I went on.

There was strict segregation of the sexes at Pitman's, the boys and girls not being allowed to sit near or speak to each other in college, and these rules were adhered to, though the odd note was passed surreptitiously. At Loreburn's, on the other hand, boys and girls could be seen openly conversing on the steps and coming and going together. Some of our students were scornful of this permissiveness, others looked on enviously.

I remember one girl, a vicar's daughter, who was anti-semitic. She had no inkling that I was Jewish with a name like Leach and always came and sat near me and talked to me. I used to wonder what kind of sermons her father preached. I found it difficult to challenge her because of the embarrassment it would cause, but began to avoid her and found more congenial company. After this experience, I always revealed my origins when such remarks were made, and they were quite rife then, before other scapegoats displaced the Jews. I often found that offenders hid their confusion by saying, 'Oh, but you're different!'

I quite enjoyed shorthand and worked at it most nights so that by the end of the term I was fairly proficient and, with the aid of a typewritter at home, developed a reasonable speed. Then I decided to look for a job.

I heard that there was a vacancy at the Dunlop Rubber Company, which then had a thriving factory in Cambridge Street. I was fortunate to be interviewed by the private secretary of the Company secretary. She was the sister of a friend of mine. The job was in the Accounts Department, so as well as tests in shorthand and typing, I was given an arithmetic test, which I found quite easy because I had done maths in matric. A day or two later, I was told that I had got the job. The principal of Pitman's was not too pleased. He had also sent one of his students for an interview and she had been at the college much longer than I had.

The Accounts Department was open-plan and all day you could see people coming and going to their offices in other parts of the factory. Two men whom I sat near made ribald remarks about some of the girls as they walked past. Sometimes I told them off, but they were a pair of entertaining characters and I could not stay annoyed with them for long.

One of them was middle-aged and wore a trilby all day to hide his bald head. The other, a young man, tall and gaunt-faced, plagued him constantly by pretending to make a grab for his hat. They talked to each other in a bantering way all the time, but I suppose it alleviated the boredom of work. The younger man was aggrieved because his fiancee, who worked at the Gas Works, earned £3 a week, while he earned only £2.10s. I earned about 30s. but I was a new girl and glad to have a job.

The head of the department was extremely handsome, and one or two of the glamour girls threw glances in his direction as they minced past in their high heels. One day his wife called in. She was surprisingly plain. Perhaps it's a subconscious wish to offset their own beauty that often causes handsome people to choose plain partners.

One of Graham Greene's short stories has always fascinated me. A very ugly couple, who live a hobbit-like existence, produce a wonderfully beautiful daughter. He made the point that only out of its extreme opposite could come such beauty.

After a few months I was moved to a smaller office, where I was to put my shorthand to use. My boss was Scottish, a very pleasant man, and I became quite infatuated with him. He had been transferred from Glasgow and had brought his secretary with him, a woman in her late thirties. She wore an engagement ring and told me that she had been engaged for fifteen years. After working with her for some time, it became obvious why the engagement had been prolonged, and why the marriage was unlikely ever to take place. She was a fussy and irritating woman.

We were extremely busy and had to work overtime, but were allowed about 1s6d. for a canteen tea. I was angry about this and usually refused the tea. It seemed poor compensation for robbing me of my leisure, but nobody else seemed to mind. One day the boss showed me a photo of his wife and child, still in Glasgow. I looked at it, and silently handed it back to him.

Sometimes I had to go into the factory with notes and letters. I felt sorry for the men who worked there. The air was foul and dust-laden. One young man used to waylay me and ask me to go out with him, but I saw in his sickly-pale face the impending doom of working in such conditions. I made excuses.

9. The Men in Black

Early in 1934 I was disturbed to learn that Oswald Mosley was to open fascist headquarters in Manchester, in Northumberland Street, in a large house not far from where I lived. On the day of the official opening, I went along to witness the event. It was obvious that quite a number of the other people present had gone along for the same purpose. Like me, they stood on the periphery, watching his supporters as they strode up the drive and mounted guard on either side of the steps while he performed the opening ceremony. There was an air of disquietude!

One day, to my surprise, I came face to face with an old school friend who, unbeknown to me, also worked at Dunlop's. She was enthusiastic about a new club she had joined called 'The Youth Front Against War and Fascism', which was situated over Syd. Abraham's garage in Waterloo Road. She asked me if I'd like to go, and I agreed.

It was a social and political club, whose members, many of them Jewish, were very concerned about the growth of fascism in Europe and particularly the way it was manifesting itself in this country under the leadership of Oswald Mosley. With rising unemployment and extreme poverty, Mosley's ranting and raving did not fall on altogether stony ground.

I went along with my friend, Freda, to the Youth Front. We climbed up the rickety wooden stairs to the large room over the garage where the meeting was to take place. I was quite impressed with the Secretary. He made a political statement on what was happening at that time and finished by drawing up a plan of action as to what we could do locally to counter the activities of the blackshirts in our area. His name was Julius Cohen, but everyone called him Jud. I found him very friendly, but unremarkable in appearance. He was of less than average height and quite stocky in build. When I asked him later in our acquaintance what made him first notice me, expecting a romantic reply, he said it was the fact that my nose was red. It was a very cold night and we had had a long walk to the club. (I drink only in moderation!)

Jud wanted to know what had made me want to join the Youth Front, and I told him that I had become interested in socialism because of some articles written by a journalist under the pseudonym of Vanoc 2nd. They appeared in the Sunday Referee, a radical paper published in the thirties. In fact I had written to him and thanked him for helping me to understand current events and asked him for a reading list. I can remember the opening sentences of his reply – 'Thanks for your thanks. I very much appreciate them.'

Among the books he suggested was Marx's "Das Kapital". I struggled with the first volume then and later at classes, but apart from learning that man's labour power is a commodity that he exchanged for other commodities, found it very hard going. Jud was intrigued when I showed him the letter, which I carried in my bag and which was by now practically in ribbons.

The Cohen family had originally lived in Blackburn, along with a small community of Jews, most of whom had fled from Russia during the pogroms. Mr. Cohen already had two daughters when he married his second wife, and she bore him seven children, six of whom survived, three boys and three girls. Mr. Cohen proved to be an inept and bad-tempered husband and father, and Mrs. Cohen, who was a shrewd business woman, ran a second-hand boot-and-shoe shop which kept the family. Occasionally there were business letters to be written and problems to be dealt with, and Jud learned at an early age to assume responsibility and act as spokesman for his mother.

When Jud started work as an errand boy in a chemist shop in Blackburn, the manager saw his potential and arranged for him to serve his apprenticeship as a pharmacist. He came to Manchester to do his final year at the University. His elder brother came with him and worked as a tailor. They shared a squalid room for a year while Jud completed his studies. As they had no money for bus fares, they ran to town every day. They were both quite fit, as they had been keen ramblers in their Blackburn days.

When Jud qualified, the family moved to Devonshire Street in Salford, about five minutes' walk from our house. It was a matriarchal domain. Though the atmosphere was easy-going, there was no doubt as to who was boss. Mr. Cohen was barely tolerated by his spouse and, for the most part, ignored by the family.

In the kitchen was a much-used couch. Sometimes it served its original function, and Mrs. Cohen ruled the roost from it in comfort. But usually it was littered with clothes. Each member of the family, as he or she came in deposited coats, scarves and gloves on it, and visitors, who were many, were encouraged to do likewise, so that the pile rose higher and higher and it was difficult to find your clothes when you left. Anyone foolish enough to leave behind an attractive coat or umbrella was unlikely ever to see it again. It was considered fair game and was appropriated and used by anyone in the family taking a fancy to it or, in the case of an umbrella, needing it.

The family lived mainly on a vegetarian diet. The kitchen cupboard was crammed with fruit, tomatoes and cheese, bananas and brown bread. There was always the chicken meal on Friday night and a few cooked meals on other days. Jud said it was fatal to praise a meal. It was served up ad infinitum until protests were made. Mrs. Cohen served her brood like a mother hen. I was indignant at the way they sat down and shouted their orders, but she didn't seem to mind.

By this time, I was tired of working at Dunlop's and began to look for a better job. I studied the Situations Vacant columns of the "Evening News" and saw that I.C.I. was advertising for typists and shorthand-typists. I thought I had more chance of obtaining a job as a typist and applied for that. I had not had much chance to use my shorthand and wasn't too confident about it. I was interviewed and offered a job in the typing pool. This was presided over by Miss Hirst, a lady with baggy eyes and a non-unpleasant manner, who assigned the girls to different departments to take dictation and type reports.

I started off under the wing of a Miss Stebbings, who was secretary to one of the big chiefs. She gave me some of her letters to type. Reading Pitman's shorthand was one thing, but Stebbings' writing was idiosyncratic and quite difficult to decipher. However, she was very good-humoured, and we used to translate her squiggles together before I attempted to do the letters.

One day Miss Hirst asked me why I had not applied for a short-hand-typist's job, as the pay was higher. I said I did not think my shorthand was good enough, but she assured me it was, and I was promoted to shorthand-typist. Then I had to take dictation from Ph.D.'s doing research work.

Most of the other girls seemed unaware of, and indifferent to, the political events of the day. One girl, in particular, denied that the Nazis in Germany had committed the atrocities that were reported in the reputable press in this country. She had friends in Germany in the

Hitler Youth Movement, which she was convinced was idealistic. The "Daily Worker", which I had started reading, was printing evidence of the links which existed between I.C.I. and its counterparts in Europe, including Germany, and I took a copy to work to show the girls, and Miss Stebbings said she would show it to her boss as she thought he would be interested. I am sure he was, though I was rather naive and did not realise that I was probably blacklisted from that time.

Jud's first invitation to go out with him made me smile. He sent quite a formal note via one of his sisters. The gist of it was, he said he proposed to see a certain film at the Rialto, and if I cared to go with him, would I meet him outside at a certain time. He was working long hours as a pharmacist, and we went to the second-house performance.

Just as we were going in, we were hailed by a member of the Youth Front. This gauche young man came and sat with us, next to Jud. At the end of the film, when Jud pointedly said to him that he was walking me home, he volunteered to accompany us. Jud, who never liked hurting anyone's feelings, agreed unenthusiastically.

We began to see each other regularly. He used to meet me every morning at the top of Northumberland Street, and walk with me to Crescent Road off Cheetham Hill Road, where I caught a works bus to I.C.I. Then he got on his bus to Queens Road where he worked in a chemist's shop.

Before he went out with me, Jud had been quite enamoured of a doctor's daughter, who went to the Youth Front. Mrs. Cohen had been pleased about their friendship. She had struggled hard to produce a chemist and expected a worthwhile return for her labours. Information had obviously gone along the grapevine and revealed that I was not likely to produce much in the way of worldly goods. My displacement a good catch was a sore disappointment to her.

One day she met me on Leicester Road and told me bluntly that she did not approve of my friendship with her son. I was shocked and angry, but did not answer her. I just walked away. I vowed I would never go to her house again.

When Jud turned up next morning as usual, I told him what his mother had said, and that, as far as I was concerned, it was all over. He just laughed and refused to take it seriously. Didn't I realise why his mother was reacting in such a way? Of course I did, but though I continued to go to the Club, I did not go to Devonshire Street for some time. Then, unbeknown to me, Cissie, whom I had told about the confrontation, went to see Mrs. Cohen and talked her round. From that time they were friends and Mrs. Cohen regarded her highly.

Jud valued the good health nature had bestowed on him. He had strong views on diet – the kind of views that are being expressed today – and soon took me in hand, saying I was not eating properly. Cissie used to cook the meal before she went out on business calls, and leave it in the oven to keep warm for us when we came home. Jud said the food value was lost and used to buy me fruit on the way to work. He said I was not getting enough vitamins.

He had one obsession that caused a lot of leg-pulling from our friends. He had inordinate faith in the healing qualities of lemons. These, he believed, were of equal value, applied externally or taken internally. He even advocated cleaning the teeth with lemon juice, and some of those gullible enough to take this advice were rewarded by the gradual erosion of their front incisors.

Jud always used scientific terminology to justify his ideas on nutrition, and the uninitiated couldn't refute them. Later, our children used to howl with anguish when their scratches and bruises were rubbed with lemon juice, but he assured them that its antiseptic qualities would vanquish any germs and would cover the wound with a kind of healing varnish. When I felt bilious, I was immediately offered the benison of a squeezed lemon and, after I'd been sick, was advised to cleanse my mouth with the same.

He never came to terms with being a chemist. He was convinced, even in his early days, that many of the drugs prescribed were harmful. He soon realised that people returning week after week with the same prescriptions had become chronic invalids. He felt that proper treatment should help to restore health. He himself made up some homeopathic remedies. One especially, a cough linctus, was very popular, and a business friend suggested he should patent it. But he had little interest in pecuniary gain. Life, for him, began when he left the shop.

When I first met Jud, he was twenty-two. At that age he had political maturity far beyond his years. He had an encyclopaedic knowledge of the historical events of this century. He had, since his teems, studied the works of Marx, Engels and Lenin, and felt that in their philosophy lay the answer to the deepening crises of capitalist society. William Morris, with his faith in an earthly paradise, combining socialist zeal with his creative activities, was to him a lode star. He used to teach classes in political economy, dialectical materialism and other aspects of Marxism, speaking to groups of workers and students. These were in Manchester at first, but later throughout the North West. He also took part in discussions and debates, sometimes with people of various political parties and religious denominations. These activities continued throughout his life.

I felt strongly attracted to him because he was the most altruistic person I had ever met. Because of his forcefulness and vitality. His care and concern for people and the way they responded to him. And because he was sensitive to my needs and feelings. But I think that if I'd realised the extent of his commitment, I'd have retreated in fright. Of all people, I came first, but I had a formidable rival – the Cause. Some women friends had to contend with lesser problems – drink, gambling or other women. It seemed as though Jud felt bound to carry the conscience of the world on his shoulders. Of such stuff are martyrs made!

Some time in 1935 we had to leave the rooms in Waterloo Road. A branch of the Young Communist League was formed, which had premises near the Griffin Hotel in Lower Broughton. At weekends we had regular sales of our newspaper, "Challenge". It was good practice for knocking on the door later, when we helped in election campaigns.

Our territory was the two-up-and-two-down terraced property in the Lower Broughton and Strangeways areas. These houses were later demolished and replaced by ill-conceived tower blocks. At least in the houses people had had easy access to each other. Often relations lived in the same street or close by. In these high-rise blocks, old people and young with families were virtual prisoners and lived a lonely existence.

It was quite unnerving going on these sales, and some of the feeble-hearted found they'd more pressing engagements and didn't turn up. The reception we got as we knocked at the doors offering our paper ranged from friendliness to extreme antagonism, sometimes with uncouth suggestions as to what we could do with it. We airily dismissed these types as lumpen proletariat and continued on our way.

We used to go to a croft on Queens Road where the Blackshirts had meetings. Their henchmen and women strutted about in their black uniforms and jack boots. Their speeches were provocative, and anti-semitic abuse was aimed at people in the crowd who looked Jewish.

Once they held a rally at the Free Trade Hall. Their stewards forcibly ejected and manhandled anyone who asked questions or heckled, causing bodily harm in some cases. The police, always present on such occasions, took no action. The blackshirts were allowed to disseminate their doctrines of hate under the guise of democratic rights, which they denied to others.

It wasn't all serious activity. Sometimes we went camping. One of the sites was Little Hayfield. It always seemed to rain, but that didn't dampen our spirits. We had campfires and sing-songs at night and visited the local pubs. We had sports days and rambles, usually in Derbyshire.

One day, returning from a ramble, we caught a train back from Hayfield. Jud and I managed to get a compartment to ourselves. We were congratulating ourselves on this when just as the train was about to leave the station, a middle-aged man opened the door and scrambled in.

After a few minutes we began to hum the chorus of one of the tunes we'd been singing with our friends on the ramble. It was a Russian revolutionary song. The words still evoke a response in me.

Then comrades face the wind
Salute the rising sun
Our country stands before the dawn
New life's begun.

To our surprise a broad smile appeared on the face of the stranger and he asked us how we knew the song. We briefly explained, and he hugged us and told us he was a member of a Russian trade delegation which was visiting Manchester. He'd been spending the day with someone in the Hayfield area and was returning to his hotel. He said he would like to take us out for a meal, but in Manchester, in those days, there was a dearth of restaurants open on Sunday, so we finished up at J. Lyons in Market Street and had tea and cakes with him.

The Spanish Civil War had a profound effect on socialists everywhere.

The fruits of victory were snatched from the popular government by the fascists under Franco, with open intervention on the part of their allies in Germany and Italy and with the connivance of the British Government. During this period, we in Salford collected money and food for Spain, the latter campaign culminating in the sending of a food ship there. Workers and intellectuals from Britain and all over the world flocked to help the republicans in their fight for a better society. Among the British were people we had known intimately, the flower of our youth. Some of them were killed with their comrades from other lands. Syd Fink was one of our particular friends who lost his life in Spain. He was in the Youth Front and later the Y.C.L. He was an extremely intelligent young man, who worked in the printing trade.

I still have a photograph of Ken Bradbury on which Jud wrote – 'Ken, a fighter for Freedom'. Jud worked for a time, when he qualified, as a locum in Chadderton where he met Ken, who was a socialist. He was training to be a compositor and lived with his parents and sister in a small terraced house. His sister had nervous trouble and Ken was Mr. and Mrs. Bradbury's pride and joy. It was painful to visit them when Ken went to Spain, and later when he died, and share in their grief. Their dignity and stoicism made a lasting impression on me.

Some of those who went to Spain returned and continued to make their contribution in trying to create a society where 'man can walk the earth so proud and free'. Those we knew included Sam Wild, Syd Booth, Maurice Levine, Cyril Bowman, Jud Clynes and many others.

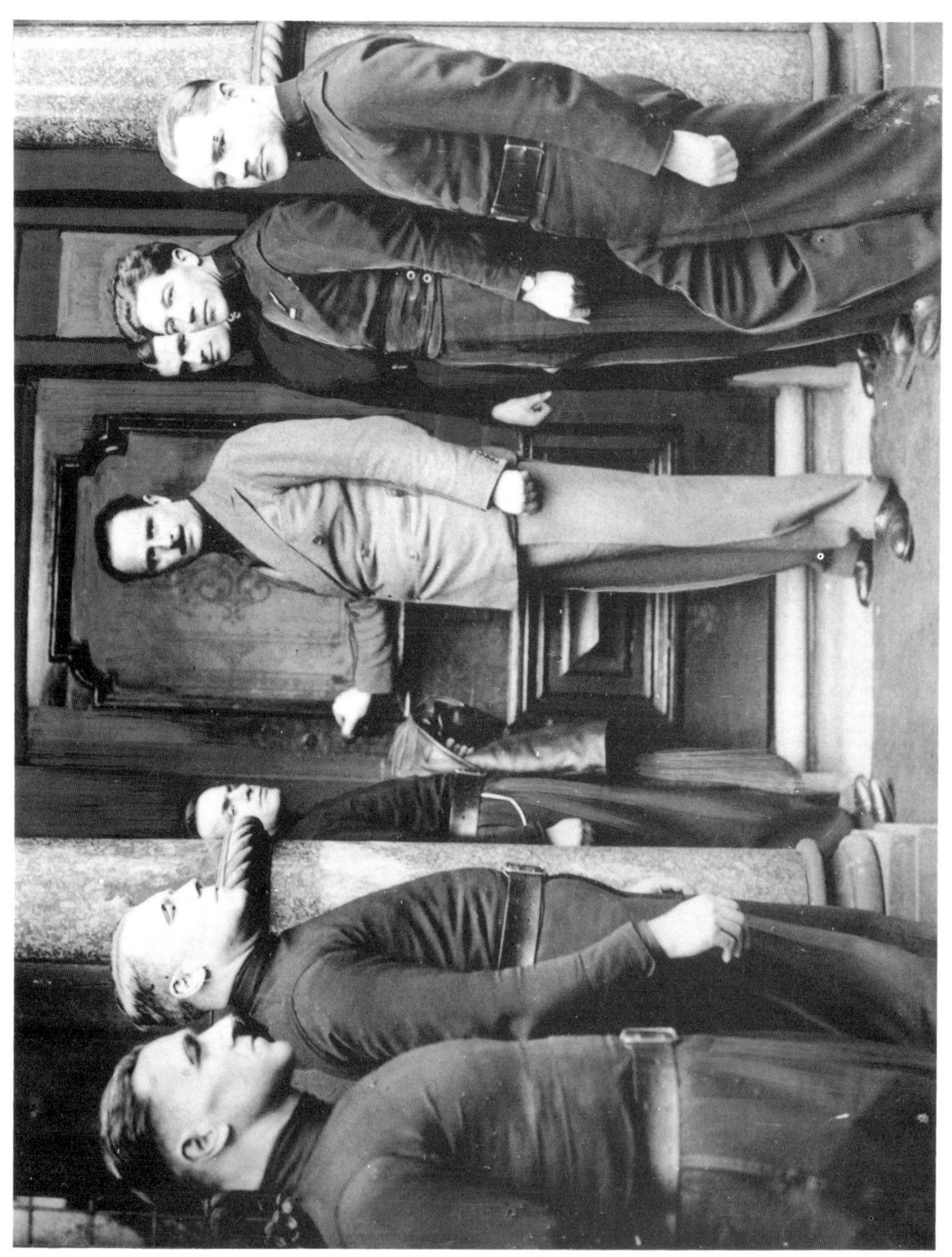

Oswald Mosley and supporters

10. Love and Politics

Jud and Hilda, Isle of Man, 1935

Marriage seemed the natural culmination of my involvement with Jud. Although I was inclined, with my new-found ideas, to dismiss marriage as a bourgeois convention, only the very brave lived together without official sanction in the thirties.

As a prelude to the impending union, we decided to get engaged when I was twenty-one and Jud twenty-four. I chose a modest ring. I think it cost £5. I was not over-keen on jewellery, but it was something to show my friends and flash at work. I watched them admiring it and assessing its value. Some time later, in an excess of zeal, when I read that Italian women, inflamed by the demagogy of Mussolini, were throwing their jewellery into his coffers, I sent my ring to the "Daily Worker" and explained why. My enthusiasm evaporated when they did not respond quickly to my noble gesture, and I wrote to them, complaining about their dilatoriness. They quickly apologised, and explained that other women had done likewise, and they had sent the jewellery to be valued!

About this time, Jud became Secretary of the British Youth Peace Council. The Chairman was the Rev. Hodgkins who lived in Crumpsall. Similar councils had been set up in various countries in Europe and America. Young people were becoming increasingly alarmed by the drift towards World War II. Affiliated to the Manchester group were Quakers, members of the Peace Pledge Union, League of Nations supporters and all the youth sections of the political parties.

Jud was the delegate from Manchester to the first conference held in Brussels. He returned encouraged by the spirit of the young people who attended, all of whom fervently wanted to avert another war. I was not over-impressed when he brought me back, as a gift, a lace-embroidered handkerchief, but he assured me the lace was hand-made and it had cost 7s 6d – a lot of money then.

I played my small part in the activities by doing quite a lot of the secretarial work involved, typing circulars and writing letters. Jud remained Secretary until we left Manchester for London in August, 1939. The last activity in Manchester was the sending of a delegate on a peace ship to America. One of the ways of raising money for this venture was the sale of book matches, which at the same time advertised the event. The matches were allocated to people from our house. When enough money had been raised and sales flagged, we were left with enough matches to last a lifetime.

We fixed the wedding date for June, 1937. I would have preferred to be married in a registry office, without any fuss, but Jud said his mother would not regard it as a proper marriage unless it was solemnised in the conventional Jewish way. We arranged to have the wedding in our house in Northumberland Street, with a local Rabbi to conduct the service.

Fortunately, the people in the house next door had recently started to do catering for festive occasions, and it was very convenient for them to move in on the day and take over. They provided a good buffet meal. The drawing room was big enough to accommodate the fifty people present. The thermal heat emanating from them ensured that, for once, the room felt really warm, though the fact that it was June did help.

In Jewish circles it was understood that the bride's parents paid for the reception. My father, with some help from Jud and myself, covered the cost, and the girls, my sisters-in-law to be, were decked out in new dresses obtained from a warehouse for the sum of 12s 6d. each. My bridal gown was somewhat more expensive. It cost 19s 11d.

Among our presents were the usual five electric irons, six bedspreads and numerous tea sets, which I systematically broke my way through during the next few years. People would have been offended then if you'd sent round a gift list.

After the reception I changed into my smart green two-piece. Jud was already resplendent in the tailor-made lounge suit his brother had made for the occasion, and off we went to "The Briars" for our honeymoon.

I knew our 'secret' was safe with the tactful Kate Ludlow. Mr. Ludlow was a different proposition. The night after our arrival, we were strolling in the garden just after supper. Darkness was falling and we could see a group of people in the lounge, looking at us through the window, not realising that we could see them, illuminated by a light at the back of the room. Mr. Ludlow was pointing a finger at us, no doubt informing them of our newly-married state.

An incident occurred when we left 'The Briars' for our journey back to Manchester which was a forewarning of the difficulty Jud had when sorting out his priorities. Mr. Ludlow took us to the station in the old Rolls Royce. There, on the platform, waiting for the same train, was a man who had been at "The Briars" that week. He would have won the prize for the bore of the week, had such a competition been organised. We spoke briefly to each other.

When the train, a non-stop to Manchester, drew up, he stepped into the nearest compartment, and I side-stepped to get into the adjacent one. Jud, who was struggling with the suitcases, was embarrassed, and called to me to follow the bore. I refused. Jud called me again and got in with him! I seethed all the way home, although I couldn't help seeing the funny side of it. I could imagine how his companion would embellish the incident to his friends! I hardly spoke to Jud for the rest of the day. He told me later that he'd worried all the way back, imagining that there might be a derailment or some such disaster.

I think one of my daughters may have inherited this trait from her father, but she was very young at the time and can be excused on those grounds. We were travelling on the top of the bus, sitting apart, because there were no double seats available. Soon the woman next to me got off and I called to Vivien to sit near me. She refused, and when I asked her why later, she said she didn't want to upset the woman next to her. The woman was a complete stranger!

The deposit for a modern semi was then about £35. Our assets were about £5, and though we could have raised the money on the strength of Jud's salary of £5 per week, we decided to rent a flat instead. We had found a nice one in the Whalley Range area, quite near to the shop where he worked.

I had been married only a few months when I discovered I was pregnant. I had been feeling unwell and consulted the doctor. I was quite dismayed at the news and he asked 'Aren't you married?' It was quite unusual to have a baby outside wedlock then. However, I explained that I was indeed married – I simply didn't want a baby at that time.

As I got used to the idea, I began to anticipate the event with pleasure rather than misgiving. Jud chose this time to produce a large carbuncle at the back of his neck. (One never hears of carbuncles these days!) It did nothing for my morning sickness to have to bathe and dress it before he went to work each day.

Jud was then working in a small busy pharmacy in Hulme with the proprietor, who needed a qualified man to cover for him. He regaled Jud with a fund of dirty jokes and Jud, being rather puritanical, began to tire of his boss's uncongenial company. He demanded a rise, which his boss was reluctant to give, so he began to look for another job.

I was doing temporary work for the Office Service Bureau in Fountain Street as I'd left ICI when I married. It was interesting but quite daunting to turn up at the Bureau and be sent to a succession of unknown assignments. I remember one small business in Deansgate where the boss dictated ungrammatical letters which I attempted to present in acceptable form. After a couple of days of arguments, I went to Fountain Street and said I refused to work there a day longer and when I told them why she said they wouldn't send anyone there again.

Because I was pregnant our upstairs flat was no longer suitable and we managed to get a council house in Chorlton. During my pregnancy I read all the baby books available. I had a profound ignorance of anything to do with babies.

Like so many people at that time I was impressed by the theories of a New Zealand pediatrician, Dr. Truby King. He has since been discredited, with good reason. He advocated strict adherence to rigid rules. The baby must be fed at regular 4-hourly intervals during the day and its crying, for the most part, ignored. It must not be allowed to disrupt the smooth running of the household.

It was a complete denial of the mother's instinct not to feed the baby if its hunger cries and searching mouth indicated it was hungry before the four hours were up. I, like so many others of that period, adhered rigidly to his dogma. Often when my baby cried, I cried with her. But I didn't pick her up. It might spoil her!

Meanwhile Jud was scouring the Situations Vacant columns of the Pharmaceutical Journal. There were few suitable openings. The biggest chain of chemists seemed to discriminate against Jewish employees.

Finally one of Jud's applications for a job was successful. It was to manage a pharmacy of Timothy Whites and Taylor in London, in the Commercial Road area. We were both keen to go to the great metropolis.

And so with some fear and trepidation, but hearts full of hope, we left Manchester for London in August, 1939. We were to return to Manchester for good less than 2 years later, but that's another story.

The Gatehouse Project publishes books written or taped by people who have reading and writing difficulties.

PUBLICATIONS LIST

AUTOBIOGRAPHIES

A GOOD LIFE: Alan 75p	ISBN 0 906253 00 4	12 pages
NEVER IN A LOVING WAY: Josie Byrnes £1.00	ISBN 0 906253 01 2	33 pages
A WOMAN ON HER OWN: Margaret Fulcher 75p	ISBN 0 096253 03 9	20 pages
THE DAYS I LIVED IN QUEEN STREET, BURY: Eric Newsham 75p	ISBN 0 906253 04 7	20 pages
RUNNING AWAY FROM HOME: Jim Hamer £1.00	ISBN 0 906253 22 5	25 pages
MY WAY OF LIVING: Carol Millbanks £1.00	ISBN 0 906253 23 3	64 pages
TOMMY, COME HOME: Thomas Murray 75p	ISBN 0 906253 02 0	20 pages

BOOKS FOR BEGINNER READERS

FUN AT FINE FARE: Paul Wilson 75p	ISBN 0 906253 10 1	16 pages
JUST MY LUCK: Frances Holden 75p	ISBN 0 906253 11 X	16 pages
TOO LATE: Frances Holden 75p	ISBN 0 906253 12 8	14 pages
KEEP YOUR HAIR ON: Frances Holden 75p	ISBN 0 906253 14 4	16 pages

COLLECTED WRITINGS

OPENING TIME, WRITING PACK: G. Frost, C. Hoy £8.00	ISBN 0 906253 13 6	14 Sections 341 pages
JUST LATELY I REALISE: £1.75	ISBN 0 906253 17 9	96 pages
WHO FEELS IT, KNOWS IT: Various £1.00	ISBN 0 906253 07 1	26 pages
TIP OF MY TONGUE: Various £1.00	ISBN 0 906253 09 8	22 pages
WHERE DO WE GO FROM HERE?: Various £1.75	ISBN 0 906253 20 9	80 pages
DAY IN DAY OUT: Various £1.75	ISBN 0 906253 19 5	39 A4 pages
WHO AM I: Various £1.00	ISBN 0 906253 13 16	35 pages
YES, I LIKE IT!: Various £1.75	ISBN 0 906253 16 0	84 pages

LOCAL PUBLICATIONS –

BETWEEN THE LINES: Monica Drury 95p	ISBN 0 906253 24 1	40 pages
THE LOVE I LOST: Doreen McLaren 75p	ISBN 0 906253 21 7	80 pages
THE BEAUMONT WRITERS' GROUP: Various 40p	ISBN 0 906253	48 pages
CHIPPING IN AT PRESTWICH: Various 75p	ISBN 0 906253 29 2	36 pages
FROM PEN TO PAPER: £1.25	ISBN 0 906253 28 4	48 pages

Orders and enquiries to:
The Gatehouse Project, St. Luke's, Sawley Road, Miles Platting, Manchester M10 8DB.
Tel: 061-205 9522.